DECA

Slade

in the 1970s

Darren Johnson

SONIC**BOND**

sonicbondpublishing.com

Sonicbond Publishing Limited
www.sonicbondpublishing.co.uk
Email: info@sonicbondpublishing.co.uk

First Published in the United Kingdom 2023
First Published in the United States 2023

British Library Cataloguing in Publication Data:
A Catalogue record for this book is available from the British Library

ISBN 978-1-78952-268-6

Typeset in ITC Garamond Std & ITC Avant Garde Gothic Pro
Printed and bound in England
Graphic design and typesetting: Full Moon Media

Follow us on social media:
Twitter: https://twitter.com/SonicbondP
Instagram: https://www.instagram.com/sonicbondpublishing_/
Facebook: https://www.facebook.com/SonicbondPublishing/

Linktree QR code:

Dedication

To my mum Joyce, for her steadfast love and support, and who was oblivious to the then-teenage Darren missing the last train home on Slade's final UK tour in 1983, necessitating a long walk in the snow and ice before finally hitching a lift for the remainder of the 32-mile journey, and still managed to give me a mighty telling off over it when the truth was finally revealed to her some 28 years later.

Acknowledgements

Following the positive reception to my first two books for the *Decades* series – The Sweet and Suzi Quatro – I was moved to begin writing about the first band I truly fell in love with: Slade. I am hugely grateful to Stephen Lambe at Sonicbond for giving me the opportunity to write a third book in the series. There is a wealth of Slade material online that I've been able to draw on for excerpts from interviews, news items and reviews – lovingly put together by dedicated Slade fans – as well as cuttings reproduced in more generic online rock music archives. However, not everything was available online – particularly some of the more brutal reviews from the end of the decade when Slade had fallen out of fashion. I was, therefore, grateful for the extensive archive of music publications maintained by the British Library to help fill in many of the gaps.

I am indebted to John Barker, Martin Brooks and Tracy Dighton for their comments on the first draft; to John Barker and Simon Putman for their assistance with the images; to Jim Lea and Don Powell for taking the time to answer my questions, and to Slade fans who shared with me their precious memories of seeing the band live.

DECADES | Slade in the 1970s

Contents

Foreword

Slade were one of the biggest bands of the 1970s. As early pioneers of what came to be known as glam rock, they enjoyed an incredible run of six UK number one singles, five top-10 albums and a succession of sold-out tours in Britain and overseas. But after a failed mid-1970s attempt at an American breakthrough, Slade returned to Britain and faced dwindling record sales, smaller concert halls and a music press that had pretty much lost interest in them. By the end of the decade, they were playing residencies in cabaret clubs and recording a cover of a children's novelty song. By the dawn of the 1980s, it all looked like it was finally coming apart. But then came a last-minute invitation to play at the Reading Festival – setting into motion a truly remarkable comeback. Another run of hits followed, until lead singer Noddy Holder finally called it a day in 1992, and Slade were no more.

This book celebrates Slade as we approach the 50th anniversary of their *annus mirabilis* – the year 1973, that saw 'Cum On Feel The Noize', 'Skweeze Me, Pleeze Me' and 'Merry Xmas Everybody' all go straight into the UK charts at number one. Every album and single of the 1970s is examined in detail, from the band's beginnings as The 'N Betweens in Wolverhampton in the mid-1960s, through each year of the decade that saw their biggest successes, with their raucous live shows and colourful media presence.

Slade came to prominence at a time of increasing solemnity in the previously-fun business of rock and roll. As culture academic, Philip Auslander put it in his 2006 study 'Performing Glam Rock: Gender & Theatricality In Popular Music': 'The primary impression psychedelic rockers apparently wished to create, was of seriousness and concentration. In keeping with the counterculture's valorisation of virtuosity, they appeared to be focused on musicianship above all, which they implied to be more important than acknowledging their audiences or creating visually interesting effects'. The dawn of the 1970s also looked like it was very much becoming the era of the album, not the single. Indeed, not long before Slade had their first hit, the very future of the single as a medium for selling rock music was being questioned. In a February-1970 *Melody Maker* article titled 'Singles: Who Buys Them', Bob Dawbarn argued: 'The singles market is now largely maintained by housewives and pre-teens, whereas the teenagers – formerly the mainstay of the singles – generally go for LPs'.

This was the era of the counterculture, long solos, virtuoso musicianship and an attachment to so-called 'authenticity', which regarded anything as vulgar as showmanship, three-minute singles and dressing up on stage, as being beyond the pale. Some saw this trend as part of the increasing class division in the once-unifying force of rock and roll. 'The psychedelic bands marked a re-polarisation of rock and pop music along class lines', argued David Simonelli – history professor at Youngstown State University – in his academic study 'Working Class Heroes: Rock Music and British Society in the 1960s and 1970s', with the largely middle-class college students seeking out the psychedelic bands (at a time when the proportion of those in higher education was much lower), and the working class kids opting for pop.

But they did not have it their own way for very long. The early-1970s saw a reaction to the counterculture's po-faced earnestness, and there was a hunger for showmanship, spectacle and singles. Enter glam rock. As Barney Hoskyns put it in a retrospective September-1998 *Vogue* piece: 'By 1972, there were two streams of glam rock – the intellectual/ art-school stream represented by Bowie, Roxy Music, Lou Reed and the nascent New York Dolls, and the shamelessly teenage one represented by Bolan, Slade, The Sweet and Gary Glitter'. However, when Hoskyns' 1972 book *Glam!* was published, he lavished chapter after chapter on the careers of Bolan, Bowie, Roxy Music and New York Dolls, while dealing with Slade's entire career in a couple of cursory paragraphs. This set the pattern for much post-1970s writing about the glam era – in both music journalism circles and academia. Fulsome praise was heaped on the more-middle-class art-school end of glam, while the likes of Slade – who were very much at the working-class end – were treated with derision or ignored altogether. As Noddy Holder told Bob Edmonds in a January 1973 interview for UK magazine *Cream:*

I'm very conscious that I'm a working-class bloke. In this business, you meet a lot of people that are not working class, and you know that you're different. Your outlook on life is different to what theirs is. You either decide you want to be part of that clique, or you don't. And I don't. I'm quite happy as I am. I don't want to move up into another sphere where I won't fit in.

Jon Stratton put it this way in his 1986 essay for the *Australian Journal of Cultural Studies*:

Glam rock had two strands – a middle-class one and a working-class one: both articulated within the same dramatic rhetoric ... Thus, for example, the music of the more middle-class strand played by Queen and Roxy Music, tended towards the pseudo-classic preoccupations which were allied to a concern with high culture. By contrast, the music of the more-working-class strand tended to emphasise the importance of dance – a reflection of the working-class-youth tradition of meeting the opposite sex at dance halls.

Slade In The 1970s is an unashamed celebration of a band at the very-boisterous, raucous, non-intellectual, non-art-school end of glam, and the story of their resilience and dogged determination to survive long after glam had fallen from favour, culminating in their spectacular return at the start of the 1980s.

Author's Note

All of Slade's 1970s studio albums, singles and their associated B-sides are examined in the corresponding chapter covering the year of their UK release. Also covered are the 1969 debut album, the two 1970s live albums and the compilation *Sladest*.

There were sometimes differences between the UK and overseas releases. The detailed reviews, tracklistings and release information in each chapter relate to UK releases. However, any relevant information on overseas releases is included in the appropriate section.

Extensive use is made of press archives and later interviews. Interview extracts carry the source credit. Any unattributed quotes are from interviews I carried out myself.

Chapter One: Beginnings

The band that became Slade evolved from a Midlands outfit called The Vendors: formed in 1963. Fronted by vocalist Johnny Howells, The Vendors invited drummer Don Powell (born in Bilston in 1946) to join. Powell pinpoints his interest in drumming as beginning with the 1961 Sandy Neilson single 'Let There Be Drums':

> It's funny how these things stick with you. It was before I was actually playing drums – it was in my youth club days when it was first released in '61. So, I'd be 14 or 15 then, and it was like the youth club, you know, playing table tennis, and we used to have the old Dansette record player, and one of the older members of the club brought this record down and it just freaked me out. I'd never heard a drumming record before – just a solo drumming record. And I thought, 'Blimey, this is incredible'.

When guitarist Johnny Shane quit The Vendors after several months, Dave Hill was invited to join, and started playing with them in January 1964. Hill was born in Devon in 1946 but relocated to Wolverhampton in early childhood. Always interested in music as a child, Hill recalled in his 2017 autobiography *So Here It Is: The Autobiography*, that his fascination with the guitar came soon after moving to secondary school, where another boy owned an acoustic guitar. Keen to encourage his son, Hill's father offered to buy him a guitar, as long as he agreed to using some of his paper-round money to pay for lessons. The guitar was eventually upgraded to an electric, and Hill played in a couple of local bands prior to the invite from The Vendors.

With Hill, The Vendors were regulars on the local live circuit, and even produced a privately-recorded four-song EP. In November 1964, they changed their name to The 'N Betweens and went on to record some tracks (unreleased) for Pye Records, and an EP for the French label Barclay. Although The 'N Betweens did not find success as recording artists, they consolidated their reputation in the Midlands as a popular live draw, and began to get bookings further afield.

On a trip to Germany for a stint at the Haberena Club in Dortmund, the band encountered Neville 'Noddy' Holder. Born in Walsall in 1946, Holder was playing guitar and singing backing vocals for Steve Brett & The Mavericks, with whom he recorded three singles. Like Hill and

Powell, Holder had developed a keen interest in music at school. In 2015, he told *Vive Le Rock's* Eugene Butcher: 'I've always been a fan of great singers. I started out singing on stage when I was seven years old, in the working men's clubs around the Black Country'.

By the time he was a teenager, Holder and some schoolmates had formed a band called The Phantoms, where he sang and played guitar. The Phantoms morphed into The Memphis Cut-Outs, and were soon gigging regularly on the local circuit, prior to being approached by singer Steve Brett, to become his backing band. After leaving Steve Brett & The Mavericks at the conclusion of their German club residency, Hill and Powell approached Holder and invited him to join The 'N Betweens. Around that time, another opportunity opened up in the band when The 'N Betweens' bass player Cass Jones announced he was leaving. 16-year-old James Whild Lea (born in Wolverhampton, 1949) was one who auditioned. Three years younger than the rest, Jim Lea was classically trained, playing violin with the Staffordshire Youth Orchestra, before the release of The Shadows' 'Apache' turned his attention to rock and roll. Prior to his audition with The 'N Betweens, he played guitar and then bass in the schoolboy group Nick And The Axeman. But, unlike his mastery of the violin, Lea was self-taught on the bass. He recalled his audition in a 2020 interview with Mark Diggins of website *The Rockpit*:

Being small and playing a bass, I couldn't get in to see any bands play in any pubs. You know, kids couldn't go into places where they sold alcohol, so that was very difficult for me. So I was self-taught and I just developed that style because I didn't have any reference point. So when I did the audition, I don't think they knew what they were looking at! It was all very fast, and I just thought, 'Well, I'm not going to just plonk along like all the other bands'. So that's what I did, I played my way, and that's why I think I got the job really – I just wasn't like anyone else. Being self-taught, I just got on with it.

The others were suitably impressed, and Lea was in. However, Hill, Holder and Powell then revealed to Lea that – far from joining a band fronted by Howells – the three were planning to go it alone with the addition of Lea on bass. A secret rehearsal without Howells was held at the Three Men In A Boat pub in Walsall and, while the band continued to honour bookings with Howells as vocalist, things came to a head in

June 1966. Howells was out of the band for good, and The 'N Betweens were now Hill, Holder, Lea and Powell.

You Better Run single as The 'N Betweens

Personnel:
Noddy Holder: lead vocals, rhythm guitar
Dave Hill: lead guitar, backing vocals
Jim Lea: bass, backing vocals
Don Powell: drums
Studio: Regent Sound, London, 1966
Producer: Kim Fowley
Release date: UK: December 1966
Chart places: UK: -

'You Better Run' (Eddie Brigati, Felix Cavaliere) b/w **'Evil Witchman'** (Kim Fowley, Powell, Hill, Holder, Lea)
Within months of forming, the revamped 'N Betweens were in the studio recording their first single. A chance encounter with eccentric US record producer Kim Fowley, led to a one-off recording contract with Colombia Records. Fowley – who was in the audience at a 29-August-1966 'N Betweens gig at London's Tiles Club on Oxford Street – was hugely impressed, and soon they were invited back down to London for a recording session at Regent Studios in Soho. Six tracks were laid down with Fowley, with 'You Better Run' selected as the A-side for the debut UK single. A pounding soul number that had been a US hit for The Young Rascals earlier that year, The 'N Betweens had recently incorporated the song into their live show. Compared to the original, it was a moodier and somewhat darker rendering. Without all the soul-infused keyboards, it was cleaner, less cluttered and – ironically (given what Slade would become famous for) – a somewhat less-frantic version than The Young Rascals' original.

The B-side 'Evil Witchman' was credited to the band and Fowley. In Powell's authorised 2013 biography *Look Wot I Dun: My Life In Slade*, he explains how the song came about: 'Kim said, 'Now we'll write a B-side together'. We'd never written before, but he took another song that we liked playing on stage: 'I Take What I Want' by The Artwoods. Kim said, 'Okay then, we'll just put new lyrics to it', and we did that. We called it 'Evil Witchman', but we all went, 'Can we call it that?'. Kim assured us, 'Yes, as long as it is the B-side, it is normal'. While it can be argued that the 'N Betweens version of 'You Better Run' was superior to the original, the same cannot be said for 'Evil Witchman', which just comes across as a cheap imitation. The other songs recorded at that session were the Otis Redding number 'Security', Dave Dee, Dozy, Beaky, Mick & Tich's 'Hold Tight', and two other songs: 'Ugly Girl' and 'Need'. 'Security' b/w 'Evil Witchman' was a US promotional single on Highland Records, and pipped the UK single by several weeks.

The press release promoting the UK single predicted a bright future for the band: 'Already, advance orders are flooding into the local record shops, and the group should be rejoicing, because if their disc is accepted as well nationally as it has been locally, then they will, without doubt, be riding high in the charts'. While the single indeed rode high in a local Midlands chart, it sold few copies elsewhere, and failed to make any national impact. The band were not helped by a stroke of bad luck that saw Listen – a rival Midlands band fronted by Robert Plant – release their own version of the song that same month. Like The 'N Betweens, Listen were signed to the Astra Agency, and receptionist Carole Williams recalled the unfortunate coincidence in Paul Rees' 2013 biography *Robert Plant: A Life*: 'At one point, I had Robert on one phone line and Noddy Holder on the other, both of them asking me which version I liked best. My loyalties were with The 'N Betweens, but I told Robert a little white lie'. Carole Williams' initial instinct was correct. The 'N Betweens' recording is by far the superior version. Unlike The 'N Betweens version, Plant alone was required for the Listen recording, with session players providing the backing. In stark contrast to the raw directness of the 'N Betweens' version, it ended up sounding rather cluttered, with an array of strings, brass and backing vocals.

Both sides of the single, the remaining songs from the Fowley session and the earlier Vendors and 'N Betweens recordings, alongside the Steve Brett & The Mavericks tracks with Holder, were eventually released on the 1996 compilation *The Genesis Of Slade*.

Despite the failure of 'You Better Run', The 'N Betweens were given an opportunity to record a follow-up, and in April 1967, found themselves at EMI's studios in Abbey Road, laying down a track called 'Delighted To See You'. But the session came to nought, and 'Delighted To See You' remained unreleased until it appeared on the 1994 compilation *Psychedelia at Abbey Road*. Unlike the earlier 'N Betweens tracks, this did not make it onto *Genesis Of Slade* and remains obscure, although it is easily found on YouTube. But the session remained memorable for the band for another reason. On the day of recording, The Beatles were in another Abbey Road studio working on the *Sgt. Pepper's* album. Holder recounted in his 1999 autobiography *Who's Crazee Now?*: 'The tracks we did there never came to anything, but it was worth it for the buzz. The Beatles were gods to every band, and we had recorded next door to them'.

If trips to the recording studio in this period were infrequent, the band's gig diary was always full, and the four worked hard to hone both their repertoire and their sound. Hill recalled in his 2017 autobiography: 'We also had a very different sound on stage – a split sound, or stereo, and that was an idea from Swin – Graham Swinnerton – a friend of ours who worked with us and helped out with gear. Rather than just hearing the bass player on one side of the stage, you could hear everything everywhere. It was really clever, and led to people saying we had such a big sound'.

In addition to constantly gigging around the Midlands – including playing support slots for the likes of John Mayall's Bluesbreakers, The Zombies, The Nashville Teens, Graham Bond and Dave Dee, Dozy, Beaky, Mick & Tich - there were frequent trips to Scotland, too. But by-far the furthest afield the band travelled was for a residency in the Bahamas. Initially contracted for eight weeks in the relative luxury of an all-expenses-paid hotel, the band later learned that not everything was as it should be, and the promoter had disappeared. In order to pay the hefty debt they had racked up, the band ended up staying for three months, living in substandard accommodation and seeing the vast majority of the money they earned being swallowed up by the hotel. However, what it *did* do for the four musicians who were to become Slade was give them endless experience in developing their stage act, many hours in one another's company bonding as a band, and exposure to much new material and musical influences from America, which neither they nor their audiences back home in Britain had heard before.

When the band eventually returned to the UK, they found a new agent – Roger Allen – who secured them an audition with Fontana Records boss Jack Baverstock. From there, the band found themselves recording not just a single but a whole album. But before its release, Baverstock insisted they change their name. After the band threw various suggestions around, Baverstock came up with Ambrose Slade. When the bemused foursome wondered what on earth this new name meant, Baverstock said it came from his secretary. Holder recalled the event in his autobiography: 'Apparently, she gave everything she owned a name … She also named everything on her desk – like her notepad, her pens, even the office stapler. I never found out what each of those objects was called, but one of them was called Ambrose, and another one, Slade'. The band had a new name, a new recording contract, a new single and their first album.

Genesis single as Ambrose Slade
Personnel:
Noddy Holder: lead vocals (B-side), rhythm guitar
Dave Hill: lead guitar, backing vocals
Jim Lea: bass, backing vocals
Don Powell: drums
Studio: Phillips, London, 1969
Producers: Ambrose Slade, Roger Wake
Release date: UK: May 1969
Chart places: UK: -

'Genesis' (Hill, Holder, Lea, Powell) b/w **'Roach Daddy'** (Hill, Holder, Lea, Powell)
Released one week before the *Beginnings* album, 'Genesis' is a band-composed instrumental. As the opening track on their debut album, it's a reasonable showcase, even if it's more than a little similar to the Fairport Convention instrumental 'Portfolio'. But as chart single material, it was an utterly ludicrous decision to release it. In 1969, an instrumental from an up-and-coming rock band was unlikely to set the charts alight. Charitably, it could be viewed as a kind of sampler – signifying, – along with the B-side – what was in store on the coming album, rather than be a serious bid for single sales. The fact that this was even considered as worthy for a single, was proof that the band needed a manager with a clear vision, and a record label who knew what to do with them. Soon they were to enjoy the benefits of both, of course, but in the meantime, 'Genesis' sank without trace.

Beginnings album as Ambrose Slade (1969)
Personnel:
Noddy Holder: lead vocals, rhythm guitar
Dave Hill: lead guitar, backing vocals
Jim Lea: bass, violin, backing vocals

Don Powell: drums
Studio: Phillips, London, 1969
Producers: Ambrose Slade, Roger Wake
Release date: UK: May 1969
Chart places: UK: -, US: -
Running time: 35:30

> *Beginnings* was more or less our live setlist, as the first album is for a
> lot of groups.
> (Dave Hill, *So Here It Is: The Autobiography,* 2017)

Following the Fontana audition, things moved pretty rapidly, and in
early-1969, the band were booked to record their first album. The
sessions took place at Phillips Studio in Stanhope Place near Marble
Arch in central London. The likes of The Who, The Walker Brothers and
Dusty Springfield recorded there, and it was later renamed Solid Bond
Studios and operated under the ownership of The Jam's Paul Weller.
Using free studio time, Slade were not given a hot-shot producer and
were left to pretty-much work things out for themselves, with just studio
engineer Roger Wake to assist them. As per Hill's above quote, they
largely set about taking songs from their live repertoire and committing
them to tape.

When glam rock emerged a couple of years later and Slade were seen
as one of the standard-bearers - along with T. Rex and David Bowie - it
was presented very much as the antithesis of late-1960s counterculture
music. As culture academic Philip Auslander argued in his 2006 book
Performing Glam Rock: Gender and Theatricality in Popular Music:
'In place of psychedelic rock's emphasis on the virtuoso electric guitar,
formulaic glam rock emphasises drums and voices as its primary
instruments. It typically features a mid-to-fast tempo foot-stomping
rhythm that remains constant throughout the song'.

But here on *Beginnings* is a band very-much immersed in the music
of the psychedelic era. Not only is there an emphasis on complex
arrangement, but the album is awash with covers of such counterculture
icons as Frank Zappa, The Amboy Dukes and Steppenwolf. It may not
be too much of a surprise that Slade would make that journey from
hippy psychedelia to glam when one considers that Bolan and Bowie
did something similar. But it's perhaps more incongruous in Slade's case,
given how much their avowedly working-class credentials and football-

terrace-style chants later characterised their music and onstage persona.

In keeping with the music's hippy vibe, the album bears an equally-psychedelic-looking cover, with the band photographed shirtless, staring at the camera, arms outstretched. One would hardly know it, but the photo was taken (in the snow) on Pouk Hill on the outskirts of Walsall in the Midlands. The band's near-freezing experience at the hands of photographer Richard Stirling was later immortalised in the song 'Pouk Hill' on the band's second album.

'Genesis' (Hill, Holder, Lea, Powell)
The album's first composition by the band, 'Genesis' is the instrumental released as a single ahead of the album.

'Everybody's Next One' (John Kay, Gabriel Mekler)
It's the first of two Steppenwolf covers on the album, both songs having also appeared on Steppenwolf's 1968 debut. Somewhat more rock and slightly less psychedelic than Steppenwolf's version, this cover is sans keyboards and puts emphasis on guitar.

'Knocking Nails Into My House' (Jeff Lynne)
Rather than being one of the songs from the US underground scene they picked up in the Bahamas, this one came from fellow Midlands outfit The Idle Race. Written by Jeff Lynne prior to his departure for The Move (and later ELO), the song had been the B-side of their 1968 single 'The Skeleton And The Roundabout'. Ambrose Slade deliver a punchy, spirited rendition, assisted (according to Powell's 2013 biography) by some realistic sound effects: 'We had blocks of wood in the studio to make Lynne's song, knocking them together to make the sound of a hammer knocking nails'.

'Roach Daddy' (Hill, Holder, Lea, Powell)
Also, on the B-side of the recent single, 'Roach Daddy', was another band composition. As was *de rigueur* for all bands who were part of the late-1960s counterculture, you simply had to have a drugs song, and this was Ambrose Slade's. Introduced to cannabis the previous year while in the Bahamas, the lyrics are pretty unambiguous:

Whatever the roach daddy
Daddy's getting high, tied to the fly, daddy

A slow, driving 12-bar blues number, it has echoes of bands like Canned Heat in terms of rhythm and lyrical content.

'I Ain't Got No Heart' (Frank Zappa)

Given that the stomping beats and sing-along choruses of early-1970s glam were seen as the anthesis of far-out psychedelia, people may be surprised by how much Slade's debut album leaned towards it, and never more so than with covers like this. In his autobiography, Hill noted: 'We heard this Frank Zappa record before most people in Britain knew who he was, and like 'Ain't Got No Heart', it really inspired us with new ideas'. Originally appearing on the 1966 Mothers of Invention debut *Freak Out*, this is a faithful cover and a fine showcase for Holder's vocal and Hill's guitar-playing.

'Pity The Mother' (Holder, Lea)

This has the distinction of being the first song to bear the Holder/Lea writing credit. Lea told Dave Kemp in the May/June-1980 edition of the *Slade Fan Club* newsletter: 'It was another of the songs that Baverstock *forced* us to write. We wrote it the day before we went down to do some recording in the studio – in Nod's parent's kitchen'. With gentle acoustic finger-picking and strident psychedelic electric guitar from Hill, mournful violin from Lea and lyrics about a mother working all hours, struggling to clothe and feed her child while her husband is away at war, the song is a world away from the likes of 'Mama Weer All Crazee Now'. While this first Holder/Lea song doesn't point to the band's future direction, it *does* suggest a successful songwriting partnership in the making, even if it was to take a while to come to fruition.

'Mad Dog Cole' (Hill, Holder, Lea, Powell)

The original Mad Dog Coll was an Irish-American mobster in 1920s New York. But according to Powell's book, this became the nickname the band used for their then-manager Roger Allen. Another instrumental, it features the simple pounding rhythm the band later deployed so effectively on singles like 'Coz I Luv You'. But Hill's lead guitar playing is still somewhat over-complicated – the trademark Slade sound yet to evolve. However, Fontana boss Jack Baverstock was suitably impressed and encouraged the band to write more. The album's other originals all emerged in the days that followed.

'Fly Me High' (Justin Hayward)
Like 'Knocking Nails Into My House', rather than being something from
an American band picked up in the Bahamas, this was from another
fellow Midlands act. This song originally appeared on The Moody
Blues' 1967 album *Days Of Future Passed*. The Ambrose Slade version
considerably toughens it, transforming the original's jaunty psychedelia
into more-conventional rock.

'If This World Were Mine' (Marvin Gaye)
This was recorded by Marvin Gaye and Tammi Terrell for the B-side
of their 1967 single 'If I Could Build My Whole World Around You'.
Ambrose Slade retain the original slow tempo, substitute the piano for
guitar, and inject some of their own rock-and-roll energy.

'Martha My Dear' (John Lennon, Paul McCartney)
Twee and whimsical at the best of times, 'Martha My Dear' originally
appeared on The Beatles' eponymous 1968 album (known as *The White
Album*). Here the song is rendered even more whimsical, with Lea's
jaunty violin-playing taking centre stage. Ambrose Slade performed the
song as part of their first TV appearance in 1969.

'Born To Be Wild' (Mars Bonfire)
The second Steppenwolf cover here is the better-known of the two, and
one that remained a staple of Slade's live set for some years. The song
was a Steppenwolf single in 1968, reaching number two in *Billboard*
that summer.

Aided by its inclusion in the film *Easy Rider*, it became a UK top-30 hit
in summer 1969. But when Ambrose Slade released their version, it was
still relatively unknown in the UK. In his book, Holder confirmed that
this was one of the songs they picked up in the Bahamas: 'Suddenly,
we had access to a huge source of new material – months before any of
our contemporaries back home. The kids were delighted to lend us their
records. We would learn songs like 'Born To Be Wild' by Steppenwolf,
then play them as requests on stage'. The band's energetic delivery
combines nicely with a hint of the trademark Holder yell that was to
help define the sound of Slade's first run of hits. It was a thrilling taste
of what was to come. Slade recorded their definitive cover of the song
a couple of years later, in front of a live audience, for the *Slade Alive!*
album.

'Journey To The Centre Of Your Mind (Ted Nugent, Steve Farmer)

Veteran American rock musician and modern-day contrarian Ted Nugent made his breakthrough as lead guitarist/vocalist with the 1960s psychedelic hard-rock outfit The Amboy Dukes. The song was the title track of their second album, and their only major hit single. It's another song Ambrose Slade picked up in the Bahamas, and their version is fairly faithful to the original. Given that the song was relatively unknown in the UK, they could at least bring a slice of classic US psychedelia across the Atlantic.

In the US, Fontana released the album with the same tracklisting, but a different title – *Ballzy* – and a different cover showing two bright red cartoon balls on a sports pitch. Neither version made the charts. In the UK, *Record Mirror* deemed the album 'a fine debut'. But in the US, Lester Bangs of *Phonograph Record* was more than scathing, calling the album 'a real dud'.

Though *Beginnings* did not sell in any great quantities, one particular visitor to the recording sessions was to have a lasting impact and be of seismic importance to the band's future. The record company were keen for the band to get a London agent, and they were introduced to John Gunnell, who was well-connected and – with his brother – ran a string of London clubs. Gunnell arranged to extricate the band from their Midlands-based-agency contract, and became their new agent. One equally well-connected friend of his was former Animals bass player Chas Chandler, who happened to come to the studio with Gunnell one day and saw Ambrose Slade in action.

Beginning his working life in the late-1950s in the Tyneside shipyards, Chandler became a semi-pro and then full-time musician, recording a string of hits with The Animals. However, on their 1966 US tour, Chandler encountered the force of nature that was Jimi Hendrix, becoming his manager and bringing him to the UK for the start of his groundbreaking solo career that same year. After producing the first two Jimi Hendrix Experience albums and overseeing the pioneering guitarist's meteoric rise, Chandler quit halfway through recording the third album, and being on the lookout for new artists to manage, he formed a business partnership with Australian entrepreneur Robert Stigwood. But he did not share Chandler's enthusiasm for Ambrose Slade, and the partnership soon dissolved.

Chandler, though was mightily impressed with the foursome from Wolverhampton. With echoes of Kim Fowley first spotting the band at the Tiles club three years earlier, Chandler hurriedly arranged to see them live in a west end London club. But this time, it would be no fleeting encounter and one-off recording venture with a maverick producer – Chandler was to remain the band's manager and producer throughout the 1970s, overseeing their rise to stardom and producing no less than six number one UK singles. In an October-1972 interview, Chandler told *Melody Maker*'s Chris Charlesworth what inspired him to sign the band: 'I went down to see them at the Rasputin Club in London, and they knocked me out. I was as impressed when I first saw Slade as I was when I first saw Jimi Hendrix. I wanted to find something different from the blues. The Animals had been mainly blues, and Jimi was the same thing, but Slade just had a ball on stage. After watching them work, I had to sign them'.

Chandler brought a new level of professionalism, and helped the band establish a clearer sense of direction. While he was a big fan of their playing, however, he was less enamoured with the band name. Shortening it was one of a number of changes he instigated early on. Hill recounted in his book: 'Ambrose Slade was a bit awkward, and he wanted something a bit more punchy. So by the end of 1969, we were just Slade'.

It was to be a time of change for a number of artists who were soon to dominate the UK charts. The Sweetshop – formed in 1968 – were obliged to shorten their name to The Sweet after a rival outfit put out a single bearing an identical band name. After releasing four albums as a hippy acoustic duo, Tyrannosaurus Rex (founded by Marc Bolan in 1967) shortened their name to T. Rex in 1970. Paul Gadd – who had several 1960s singles under the name Paul Raven – began recording as Gary Glitter in 1971, while the Boston Showband – who had worked with Gadd/Raven – morphed into The Glitter Band, the backing band for the now-disgraced and discredited singer before breaking out to have their own hits.

There was also to be a drastic change of image for Slade. Struggling to attract the attention of the music press, and aware of the growing column inches that were being devoted to the newly-emergent and increasingly-notorious skinhead youth subculture, band publicist Keith Altham hit on the idea of turning Slade into a skinhead band. While bands like Small Faces had their roots in mid-1960s mod culture, and few would disagree that bands like the Grateful Dead were *bona fide* hippies, Slade had zero affiliation with the youth cult it was suggested they represent. Nevertheless, Chandler was enthusiastic about Altham's plan, so the band were dispatched to the barbers to have their long locks shorn, and were then taken shopping to be kitted out with boots and braces. None of the band were enthusiastic about the ruse, but at the same time, they were reluctant to do anything to jeopardise the situation. Powell told Lise Falkenberg in *Look Wot I Dun*: 'We were a bit scared, because we thought that if we said no, Chas probably wouldn't want to manage us anymore. Now we had finally found someone who was a proper manager, and we were to lose him because of a haircut?'. But one person who *did* approve of the new look was Powell's mother. The drummer told *Rolling Stone* in 1973: 'She was thrilled at the idea of having a neat short-haired son!'. An October-1969 interview with *Record Mirror* saw Lea come across as perhaps the least-convincing skinhead ever: 'All this *aggro* is built up by the press. And hippies, well, they don't work. They're alright I suppose, they're a different thing again. They're part of our audience'. The interviewer (Rob Partridge) then moved on to football: 'That's the sort of thing I mean about being built up by the press – I don't even like football'. After questioning Lea about the band's image, Partridge delved into their musical influences: 'Someone in the room put the Slade's first single 'Wild Winds Are Blowing' on the record player. It is heavy rock music, not reggae or anything else we had been led to expect from skinheads. So, I asked Jim about his musical influences, and guess what? – not Desmond Dekker or Prince Buster or any West Indian, but *Eric Clapton* was number one'.

The band's first release in skinhead mode – and credited to The Slade rather than the more obvious Slade – was the non-album single 'Wild Winds Are Blowing'.

Wild Winds Are Blowing single as The Slade

Personnel:
Noddy Holder: lead vocals, rhythm guitar
Dave Hill: lead guitar, backing vocals
Jim Lea: bass, backing vocals
Don Powell: drums
Studio: Olympic, London, 1969
Producer: Chas Chandler
Release date: UK: October 1969
Chart places: UK: –

'Wild Winds Are Blowing' (Jack Winsley, Bob Saker) b/w **'One Way Hotel'** (Holder, Lea, Powell)

In his 1999 autobiography, Holder explained how the single came about: 'Chas met up with us one day and said, 'I've found a song that's perfect for Slade'. He had been sent it by a publishing company. It was a good pop/rock song, not too commercial. It was really our first proper single'. Despite the title – and in stark contrast to later singles – the idea of wildness is only really hinted at here, rather than being the *modus operandi*. But it's a catchy number, and was to become much better-known to fans when it appeared on the number one-selling 1973 compilation *Sladest*.

The B-side 'One Way Hotel' was a band composition. The evocative, grimy kitchen-sink realism was a world away from the likes of 'Cum On Feel The Noize', but it revealed Powell to be a promising lyricist – his lyrics becoming an essential component in this early period. Recalling the inspiration for 'One Way Hotel', the band said in the *Sladest* liner notes: 'There were the four of us plus two roadies, in one hotel room. Six beds. It was pouring with rain and we were skint – not even the price of a pint between us'. A slightly reworked version of the song appeared on the *Play It Loud* album the following year.

This recording was the first of many visits to Olympic Studios in Barnes. Established in 1966 – in a building that at various times had been a music hall, cinema and TV studio complex – Olympic became a favourite for the likes of The Rolling Stones and The Who. Chandler had recorded Hendrix there, and Olympic would become Slade's home away from home for the first half of the 1970s. All of their big glam-era hits – except for 'Merry Xmas Everybody' – were recorded here.

'Wild Winds Are Blowing' failed to chart, but it was clear that Chandler's connections were opening up new opportunities for the band. Slade made their first national TV appearance on *Monster Music Mash* – the show hosted by Chandler's former Animals bandmate Alan Price. Broadcast on 4 November 1969, Slade performed the new single and their version of 'Martha My Dear'. In his book, Holder made much of the incongruous sight of a bunch of skinheads performing the Beatles song on national television: 'It's the one clip that's always shown when TV programmes do those before-they-were-famous spots'. There was also a BBC studio session for Radio 1, broadcast on 10 November. Likewise, the furore over the skinhead publicity stunt at least ensured that the music press picked up the single, even if the reviews weren't entirely favourable. Penny Valentine reviewed the single for *Disc*:

> If they are supposed to be more than just a group cashing in on a fad, then one expects a whole new revolutionary sound on record, just as The Who presented us with in the days when they presented the mods. 'Wild Winds Are Blowing' has a faintly aggressive vocal with a *heavy* backing. Nothing particularly stunning; no real *aggro* voice, and nothing to wake you from the Sunday afternoon boredom or get you leaping off to football in your hobnail boots!

Even if the skinhead look was an odd fit that drew press suspicion, and even though the music never quite matched it, the band were starting to get noticed. With a new manager, a new name and a growing level of confidence, Slade could enter the new decade in a far stronger position than they had been a year before.

Chapter Two: 1970 – Playing It Loud

1970 would not be the year of Slade's commercial breakthrough, but a number of things would begin falling into place. Already a talented band, Chandler helped to professionalise them. His management and production skills – together with his many connections inside the music industry – would mean that Slade not only began to sound better than ever, they would start to get noticed more too. 1970 would see their first appearance on *Top Of The Pops* as well more appearances on other TV shows. Encouraged by Chandler, they would also begin writing more of their own material, with nine of the coming second album's 12 tracks being originals. But the year's first single would be another cover.

Shape Of Things To Come single
Personnel:
Noddy Holder: lead vocals, rhythm guitar
Dave Hill: lead guitar, backing vocals
Jim Lea: bass, backing vocals
Don Powell: drums
Studio: Olympic, London, 1970
Producer: Chas Chandler
Release date: UK: March 1970
Chart places: UK: –

'Shape Of Things To Come' (Barry Mann, Cynthia Weil) b/w 'C'Mon, C'Mon' (Holder)
'Shape Of Things To Come' originally appeared on the soundtrack of the cult 1968 coming-of-age film *Wild In The Streets*, where it was performed by the fictitious band Max Frost and the Troopers. Slade take the original's moody, Doors-like psychedelia, gave it a harder, more-aggressive edge and turned it into a pre-glam Slade anthem.

The B-side, with the glam-sounding title of 'C'mon, C'mon' (a phrase that would later be utilised by Mike Leander and Gary Glitter) is an energetic rocker. With its no-nonsense, yelled chorus, Holder's lyric represented a different style to that of Lea and Powell, and pointed the way to the songs Slade would soon become synonymous with.

Although the single did not chart, media publicity was significant, and the band bagged their first appearance on the BBC's *Top Of The Pops* on the 2 April edition of the show, as well as on the BBC music series

Disco 2 a couple of weeks earlier. The *NME* deemed the single a 'rip-roaring rocker'. The review praised the band's 'abundant musical ability' and the single's 'thunderous beat and raucous guitar sounds', making comparisons with the early days of The Who.

This was the band's final single on the Fontana label, though the song was included on Slade's first Polydor album released later in the year.

Slade were now frequent visitors to the BBC radio studios at Maida Vale. At the time, BBC Radio DJs were restricted in the airtime they could devote to playing records, necessitating the broadcast of specially-commissioned studio sessions by a variety of artists. Slade were one such band, performing their first session for the BBC in 1969, but by 1970 they were being called on regularly. BBC sessions that year not only included renditions of Slade's own material (like 'See Us Here' and 'Know Who You Are', which would soon appear on their second album) but covers of material by artists as varied as Delaney & Bonnie, Moby Grape, The Moody Blues, Traffic, The Beatles and Fairport Convention. Many of these sessions eventually appeared on the excellent 2009 Salvo double CD *Slade Live At The BBC*. It remains one of the most significant Slade releases beyond their original albums, and is a crucial addition to any Slade collection.

Know Who You Are single
Personnel:
Noddy Holder: lead vocals, rhythm guitar
Dave Hill: lead guitar, backing vocals
Jim Lea: bass, backing vocals, violin (B-Side)
Don Powell: drums
Studio: Olympic, London, 1970
Producer: Chas Chandler
Release date: UK: September
Chart places: UK: –

'Know Who You Are' (Hill, Holder, Lea, Powell) b/w **'Dapple Rose'** (Lea, Powell)
Although Polydor was established in Germany in 1913, by the early-1960s, it had come under the Phillips-Siemens empire, thus sharing the same parent company as the Fontana label. However, Chandler believed Polydor was a better fit for Slade, so he negotiated what was basically

an internal transfer within the corporate structure, and the band began recording for Polydor, which they were to do until the late-1970s.

Chandler was keen to encourage the band to write more of their own material, and in sessions for the forthcoming *Play It Loud* album, they got the idea to add vocals to their instrumental 'Genesis'. Powell was assigned to come up with the lyrics. There are clear references to Hill in the song: 'H sing a song to make out that your playing is easy'. Rather than re-record the entire thing, the original instrumental track was repurposed with Holder's vocal added.

The B-side 'Dapple Rose' was a melancholy song about an old neglected horse. In a 2009 Q&A for the www.slayed.co.uk fan forum, Powell was asked about the song's inspiration: 'I've always had a fondness for horses, and where I lived with my parents, there were some fields over the back and there were always gypsies camping there. They used to have these horses and donkeys, and they always looked dead to me. They were not looked after, which was sad'.

As with the two previous Chandler-produced singles, 'Know Who You Are' was another flop. But Chandler's standing in the industry and the continuing furore over the band's newfound skinhead image ensured that, once again, there was a decent amount of publicity. There was another TV slot on *Disco 2* – where the band performed 'Know Who You Are' and 'Sweet Box' from the forthcoming *Play It Loud* album. The single also picked-up reviews in several of the main music papers. *NME* decreed the song to be 'a hard-hitting piece of philosophy with a walloping beat', while *Record Mirror* believed the song had 'chart chance'. But that prediction proved to be inaccurate. The single sold poorly, and Polydor soon deleted it, causing it to become a lucrative collector's item in later years. However, the live version of 'Know Who You Are' on the monster-selling *Slade Alive!* album 18 months later, finally ensured the song had a receptive audience.

Play It Loud album (1970)

Personnel:
Noddy Holder: lead vocals, rhythm guitar
Dave Hill: lead guitar, backing vocals
Jim Lea: bass, violin, backing vocals
Don Powell: drums
Studio: Olympic, London, 1970
Producer: Chas Chandler

Release date: UK: November 1970
Chart places: UK: -, US: -
Running time: 34:05

> With that album, we were too concerned with arrangements and
> stuff. We wouldn't get involved in all that now. We don't like anythin'
> complicated these days.
> Noddy Holder reflecting on *Play It Loud* in a July 1973 *NME*
> interview with Nick Kent.

Other than the one-off session with Kim Fowley four years earlier,
having Chandler at the helm was the band's first real taste of working
with a producer. The whole album was recorded at Olympic Studios
in West London and while it was still a long way from the sounds that
would characterise the band's early hits, Chandler's influence was
making its presence felt. The music tended to be more punchy and
direct than on the first album – the psychedelic influence was gradually
waning, and there were far fewer covers than on the debut.

 Though the album title hints at the trademark stomp that the band
would soon become known for, the cover art is about as far from glam
rock's colourful theatrics as it was possible to get. Their hair had grown
slightly longer, and they no longer sported the skinhead gear worn
at the time of the 'Wild Winds Are Blowing' photo shoot, but Slade
certainly did not look like most other rock bands around at the time.
The combination of the sepia cover, cobbled street and Holder's flat cap,
gave the appearance of the four having somehow landed in 1970 from
another age entirely.

'Raven' (Lea, Holder, Powell)

With Lea and Powell having become quite prolific songwriters by this
point (Lea on music and Powell on lyrics), 'Raven' is one of several
Lea/Holder/Powell songs on the album. Powell explained in his 2013
biography: 'Nod finished a lot of the songs lyrics-wise. I can write
lyrics, but back then, Jim and myself couldn't finish the songs, so we'd
take them to Nod to have him help out'. A punchy number with a
slightly left-field lyric, 'Raven' pretty much establishes the template for
the album. There are no crazee mamas or noizy crowds going wild,
wild, wild here. Instead, we have a song about the behavioural traits of
corvid birds.

'See Us Here' (Lea, Holder, Powell)
This heavy, brooding track, with its ominous bass line, sees Holder
growing in confidence as a vocalist – belting out Powell's lyric, which is
a reflection on the band's rise to prominence.

> See us here, see us there
> Pick us out anywhere
> Take a look we're everywhere

Though they were yet to have a hit, the band were attracting more
media attention and starting to be noticed and talked about.

'Dapple Rose' (Lea, Powell)
This was the 'Know Who You Are' B-Side.

'Could I' (Jimmy Griffin, Robb Royer)
While the covers on the debut album largely came from the band's
live repertoire, the two covers here were at the instigation of Chandler
and his erstwhile Animals bandmate and business associate John Steel.
'Could I' was a song from the debut album of US MOR combo Bread,
and Steel sourced it for inclusion on *Play It Loud*. Slade put their own
stamp on it, and it fits the album well.

'One Way Hotel' (Lea, Holder, Powell)
The 'Wild Winds Are Blowing' B-side has a slightly different mix on the
album, with some of Hill's jazz-like guitar licks toned down. This was
consistent with Chandler's view that from now on the band needed to
forget the complex arrangements and go for more-simple and gutsy
playing.

'The Shape of Things to Come' (Mann, Weil)
The Fontana single from earlier in the year.

'Know Who You Are' (Lea, Holder, Powell, Hill)
Released as a single that autumn, this song was Hill's only writing credit
on the album, thanks to him been involved in the writing of the original
instrumental when it was known as 'Genesis'. Hill later said in his book
that he had a certain amount of frustration with the band not taking
up his songwriting ideas, but at this early stage he was content that his

guitar-playing and onstage showmanship were his contribution to the band's unique chemistry.

'I Remember' (Lea, Powell)

The song has lyrics from Powell about a man losing his memory:

> That the fire in the grass
> It just wiped out my past
> And my memory's gone

It was oddly prophetic, given that just three years later, Powell would find himself in a similar situation. As he recalls in *Look Wot I Dun*: 'In hindsight, it is spooky that I would write a song about a man who loses his memory, three years prior to the accident where I got amnesia. I don't even remember what the inspiration was at the time'. The lyric might be introspective and philosophical, but the band pass up the chance to give the song a gentle psychedelic twist like they might have done a year before, and instead deliver it with speed, power and unrelenting fury.

'Pouk Hill' (Lea, Holder, Powell)

Named after the location of the debut album cover's photo shoot, this song is certainly no paean to a local beauty spot on behalf of the West Midlands Tourist Board, but instead recalls the misery of that day spent bare-chested in the snow in sub-zero temperatures:

> We were there, standing bare
> With our arms in the air
> Did you see us?

It is one of the album's slower songs, and whatever were the band's memories of that particular day, Holder delivers the lyric with a bittersweet, melancholy air rather than with undisguised fury.

'Angelina' (Neil Innes)

If the band Bread were an unexpected source of material, the album's other cover version has an even-more left-field pedigree. 'Angelina' was written by Neil Innes of the Bonzo Dog Doo-Dah Band, The Rutles and the BBC TV series *The Innes Book Of Records*. Originally released in

1970 by Innes' post-Bonzos outfit The Word, Slade gave the originally slow and Lennon-esque piano ballad a much heavier treatment.

'Dirty Joker' (Lea, Powell)

Two more Lea/Powell originals round off the album. Raw and gritty but with an uncharacteristic funky riff, 'Dirty Joker' is another song with a semi-autobiographical lyric from Powell, focussing on the band's rise to prominence and their inevitable hangers-on. Perhaps pre-empting the rise of the glam chorus, handclaps appear in the middle instrumental section.

'Sweet Box' (Lea, Powell)

The final track is one of the album's real highlights. Of all the tracks on *Play It Loud*, it most closely points towards the archetypal Slade song – combining melody, simplicity, power and punch. Though Holder was soon to replace Powell in the lyric department, Powell excelled himself in his inspirations for this one, with the opening line 'Five! Shade! Six! Size! Cut! Out!' coming from a dressmaking pattern!

Reviewing the album in December 1970, *NME* defined it as 'aggressive', arguing that 'The lead vocalist is inclined to shout too much. But then, maybe that is the appeal of the group'. Despite having a big-name producer, being on a new record label and attracting growing media interest, the album failed to have chart impact. It reached the top 40 in Canada three years later, but there was no immediate success for it.

Concert-wise, 1970 had been a busy year for Slade, with around 100 gigs. With a heavy focus on the West Midlands, bookings were still the typical mix of hotel function rooms, community centres and youth clubs that had dominated their schedule the year before. A December-1970 *Derby Evening Telegraph* review enthused about the 'ex-skinhead group who had to change their name to get bookings'. Richard Cox wrote, 'The true sounds in progressive rock, hit Derby like never before on Friday, and left everyone at the Great Hall, Kedleston Road, wondering if it was all really true'. But signs of more prestigious venues were appearing on the horizon, with several gigs at London's Marquee Club, and support slots around the country for the likes of Arthur Brown, Fat Mattress, Gentle Giant and Blodwyn Pig.

But it was still a long, hard slog. By the end of 1970, Chandler had been Slade's manager for almost two years, also producing an album and three singles. But though he never lost his faith in the band, there was clearly frustration with there still being no sign of a hit. This was in stark contrast to Jimi Hendrix, who had signed a contract with Chandler in September 1966, and within three months, was enjoying chart success with 'Hey Joe'. Slade were hoping that 1971 would finally bring that long-awaited commercial breakthrough.

Chapter Three: 1971 - Getting Down With It

After five years together, hundreds of gigs, several flop singles and two albums, 1971 would be the year Slade finally made their big breakthrough. Not only would they enjoy their first hit that summer with 'Get Down And Get With It', but their self-written single 'Coz I Luv You' released that autumn would go all the way to number one.

The band's short-lived skinhead image was now beginning to evolve. Their hair slowly grew out, and the stage clothes gradually became more flamboyant. In his autobiography, Hill recalls a pivotal moment in February 1971 when Slade went to see Mott The Hoople play at Wolverhampton Civic Hall: 'They had this slightly hippie thing going on where they had their trousers tucked into knee-length boots – which was unusual, because mostly back then it was flares down over your shoes'. Hill began incorporating that look for his own on-stage image. Holder, meanwhile, noted in his book: 'Our hair was growing down at the back on to our collars like the skinhead girls, and we were wearing colourful clothes instead of the jeans and the Ben Sherman shirts'.

Though recorded in spring 1971 and released in May that year, the band's first hit 'Get Down And Get With It' did not reach the top 40 until well into the summer. Therefore, the first half of 1971 carried on pretty much as before. Live gigs were a typical mix of rock clubs, colleges and ballrooms, and there were a handful of one-off support slots for the likes of Atomic Rooster, Argent and Keef Hartley. But one song, in particular, was going down fantastically well live, giving Chandler a clear idea of what the band's next single should be.

Get Down And Get With It single

Personnel:
Noddy Holder: lead vocals, rhythm guitar
Dave Hill: lead guitar, backing vocals
Jim Lea: bass, backing vocals
Don Powell: drums
Additional personnel:
Zoot Money: piano
Studio: Olympic Studios, London, 1971
Producer: Chas Chandler
Release date: UK: May 1971
Chart places: UK: 16, US: -

'Get Down And Get With It' (Bobby Marchan) **b/w 'Do You Want Me'** (Hill, Holder), **'Gospel According To Rasputin'** (Hill, Holder)

Almost every Slade fan knows the band had their first hit with a Little Richard cover. But 'Get Down And Get With It' – far from being from the early rock-and-roll era of 'Tutti Frutti' and 'Long Tall Sally' – was from a later stage in Richard's career. His version was released in February 1967 but did not chart on either side of the Atlantic. In fact, the Bobby Marchan song began life in 1964 when he released it as a soulful R&B number with stacks of brass. Little Richard brought his own indomitable personality and trademark pounding piano to the song, and it was that version which encouraged Slade to add it to their live set, where it became a barnstorming show closer. But it was Chandler's idea to record it. Powell recalled in *Look Wot I Dun*: 'We used to finish our shows with it, and then Chas said, 'It goes down so well on stage that it's gonna be your next single''.

Capturing the raucous energy of their live act, Slade took Little Richard's version, lost the sax and powered it up with hard-rocking guitar. Lea recalls the recording session: 'There was something about the four of us playing when we were on stage. And we went to that big studio at Olympic ... we always went to that studio because it was like doing a gig, and we were comfortable with that because we were really bloody good'. Chandler brought in session player Zoot Money to provide the pounding piano accompaniment, and – in a stroke of genius that proved to be highly significant – he decided the single needed some overdubs. Holder recalled in *Who's Crazee Now?*: 'There was a big stairwell outside the studio which was really echoey. We set the mics up out there, then recorded the four of us clapping our hands and stamping our feet'. Not only did this help define the Slade sound, but the pounding and stomping became a hallmark of glam rock in general – as intrinsic to the very essence of glam as the moment Marc Bolan put glitter on his cheeks earlier that year.

The B-side had two Hill/Holder songs. The first – 'Do You Want Me' – was slow, brooding and sexually charged and provided a contrast to the fast and furious A-side, although the confident trademark Holder yell was clearly in place at this point. The second track was 'Gospel According To Rasputin'. The Russian mystic and friend of the Romanovs was clearly a popular choice for song lyrics in the 1970s. This was no Bony M -style singalong, though. With big vocal harmonies and a multifaceted arrangement, this was still Slade very much in heavy progressive mode – in stark contrast to the pounding simplicity of glam.

NME's Chris Welch was in no doubt that the single would be a hit: 'Here, Slade's Noddy bellows a belligerent rocker, and there is a foot-stamping chorus that *ensures* it a place in the chart'. Over at *Sounds* (which had been set up by former *Melody Maker* journalists the previous year, and very much saw itself in the vanguard of *serious* rock music), reviewer Penny Valentine was less than impressed: 'Good heavens. A most peculiar title, as Mrs. Whitehouse would be the first to admit. Slade rock and bash their way through this track with great spirit, but to my untutored ears, end up sounding like rocking chipmunks'.

The single slowly picked up airplay, and the band played the song live on *Whittaker's World Of Music* (hosted by Roger Whittaker) the week the single was released. But it took time to break through, and there was also a legal problem to be rectified. When first released, the A-side had been erroneously credited to Holder/Lea/Hill/Powell /Penniman (Penniman being Little Richard's real name), rather than the actual writer Bobby Marchan. After lawyers got in touch, it was hurriedly re-released on 8 June credited to Marchan, with no attempt this time to claim a band co-writing credit.

Nevertheless, the single slowly crept up the charts, breaking into the Top 50 on 19 June at number 45, nudging up to 43 the following week, and reaching 32 on 10 July: which meant an appearance on *Top Of The Pops* the following week. Hill reflected: 'We went on *Top Of The Pops*, and that really was the start of something else, the next phase of Slade'. Eventually peaking at 16 on 21 August, there was further *Top Of The Pops* exposure, but the producers utilised a promo video or scenes of the studio audience dancing to the track. However, the band were to return to the show with many subsequent hits. Moreover, given that the record was a hit in a handful of other European countries, there were TV appearances in Switzerland, and the Netherlands where the single went all the way to number four.

Hill's ever-more-bizarre sartorial choices were to establish an unforgettable template for glam's visual side. But glam wasn't just about image, it was about sound too. With foot stomps, handclaps, raucous but simple guitar riffs, sing-along choruses and homages to rock and roll's 1950s glory days, Slade helped define the archetypal *sound* of glam rock, not just the look. In this regard, glam rock was as much a studio production technique as it was a visual medium. Chandler, in particular, should be credited for the part he played in creating the sound of glam, a sound that numerous other producers of the glam era would take their cues from.

Though Marc Bolan and T. Rex had begun making the journey from hippy acoustic duo to fully-fledged glam-rock outfit some months earlier (via the singles 'Ride A White Swan' (1970) and 'Hot Love' (1971) – it's important to remember how much Slade were early pioneers at this stage. The Sweet began having hits in 1971 but were still very much a bubblegum pop act, taking musical cues from the likes of The Archies and The 1910 Fruitgum Company. It would be well into 1972 with their 'Little Willy' and 'Wig-Wam Bam' singles before The Sweet developed anything approaching glam rock. Gary Glitter and his producer Mike Leander had their first hit with 'Rock And Roll' (Parts 1 and 2) in summer 1972, and even Bowie did not launch his Ziggy Stardust persona until 1972.

So, like Bolan a few months earlier, Slade's look and sound found a receptive audience. But why did glam take off when it did? A number of culture academics have described the rise of glam rock as a direct response to psychedelia. In *Glam Rock: Music In Sound And Vision*, Simon Philo pinpoints the transition from traditional rock and roll's fun hedonism to serious counterculture rock, to the summer of 1965 and the success of Bob Dylan's 'Like A Rolling Stone': 'Henceforth, the joyous inarticulacy that characterised rock 'n' roll would largely be confined to pop. Rock, by contrast, would seem to favour the joylessly articulate'. Glam emerged as a colourful riposte to all that. Philip Auslander argued in *Performing Glam Rock: Gender & Theatricality in Popular Music,* (2006), 'In many ways, psychedelic rock and glam rock are polar opposites. Whereas psychedelic rock emphasised musical virtuosity and seriousness, glam rock emphasised accessibility and fun. If psychedelic rock was suspicious of spectacle and theatricality, glam rock celebrated those aspects of performance'.

Academic hindsight is a wonderful thing, of course, but the band themselves expressed similar sentiments at the time. Having finally had their breakthrough hit, there was renewed interest from the music press. In a July-1971 *NME* piece by Roy Carr titled 'Slade: Bovver Boys Who Grew Their Hair And Got A Hit', Hill stated the band's philosophy: 'I think people wanna start dancing again. It's still all down to having a good time ... we can see it when we're on stage. As soon as we start bashing it out, everyone starts leaping about'. In the same interview, Holder reflected on the folly of the band's skinhead dalliance: 'Things got to such a point, that other bands wouldn't even share the same dressing room with us'.

The skinhead crops might have been growing out, but by early-1970s standards, their hair was still pretty short. In a July-1971 letter to the *NME*, readers Julie Morrisson and Denise Jones wrote in the band's defence: 'We are referring to the apparent victimisation of Slade purely because their hair is short. We fail to see how three inches or more of hair can fail to make the group acceptable. Surely the group should be judged on their musical ability – of which Slade have plenty – and *not* by the length of their hair'. Musical ability, the band clearly had an abundance of. But the next big test would be songwriting ability. The pressure was on to come up with a follow-up hit, and this time Chandler would be urging the band to write their own.

Coz I Luv You single

Personnel:
Noddy Holder: lead vocals, rhythm guitar
Dave Hill: lead guitar, backing vocals
Jim Lea: bass, violin, backing vocals
Don Powell: drums
Studio: Olympic, London, 1971
Producer: Chas Chandler
Release date: UK: October 1971
Chart places: UK: 1, US: -

'Coz I Luv You' (Holder, Lea) b/w **'My Life Is Natural'** (Holder)
More pop-orientated than the rock-and-roll raunch of 'Get Down And Get With It', 'Coz I Luv You' had a different feel altogether. Importantly, it also represented the real start of the phenomenally-successful Holder/Lea songwriting partnership. Interviewed by this author in 2018, Lea explained how it came about:

We'd had 'Get Down And Get With It' as our first hit, and it was about coming up with the next one. Because 'Get Down And Get With It' was an everybody-join-in type thing, I thought, to write something like that is just going to be a cop-out. So, I thought about bridging the fact that we were going to make a pop single, with trying to make it a bit gritty as well. So, I came up with (sings melody) and I got my acoustic guitar and I went over to Nod's. I'd never written with Nod before, and really it was like trying to get the singer on board, so it's kind of political in case it was a 'Well, I don't want to do anything with a violin'. That's what could've happened, but it didn't. And we worked on the 'I just like the things you do' bit, and obviously, I knew that this was going to be really big.

Chandler was immediately convinced that the pair had written a huge hit, and was keen to record it as soon as possible. Concerned it might be too lightweight for Slade, they and Chandler set about *Sladifying* it. Handclaps and stomping were added to the irresistibly-catchy melody: with stunning results. Holder told Mark McStea in a 2019 interview for *Vive Le Rock*: 'We thought it was a decent pop ditty! We really worked on bringing it to sound more like our first hit, 'Get Down And Get With It', with the claps and the foot stamping'. The only other thing to consider was the title. Originally titled 'Because I Love You', there was concern that it looked far too wimpy for Slade, until Holder had the idea of spelling it how he sang it. The title became 'Coz I Luv You', and misspellings then became a trademark feature of Slade's glam-era hits.

The B-side – Holder's 'My Life Is Natural' – alternated between light acoustic passages and Powell's powerhouse drumming, which heralded the start of heavy-as-hell guitar-driven interludes. It was a complete contrast to 'Coz I Lov You'. Holder's somewhat mysterious lyric contemplating the nature of good and evil, was furiously delivered throughout.

Reviewing 'Coz I Luv You' for *NME*, Chris Welch was optimistic: 'After their last screaming rocker, here is some more foot-stomping music from an ever-popular band who have brought dancing back to modern rock; nice bass line and mysterious effects along the way; top ten and no problems'. The single did better than that, though. Chandler's prediction that Holder and Lea had written a chart-topper, proved to be entirely correct. It was released on 8 October 1971, and by the end of the month, it entered the UK chart at 26, shot up to eight a week later, and the following week began a four-week run at number one. There was a succession of *Top Of The Pops* appearances in late October, November and early December. Lea explained: 'It's only recently where people have said, 'I saw Jim Lea from Slade with an electric violin playing on *Top Of The Pops*, and that's why I started playing violin'. And you know, it's really edifying to think that you might've set some trail for something that happens in the future'. Given the success of the single elsewhere (number one in Ireland, two in the Netherlands, seven in Australia and Belgium, and nine in Germany), there was a string of overseas TV appearances, including chart shows in France, the Netherlands and Germany, with a stunning live performance for Germany's *Beat Club*.

In the second volume of Holder's memoirs – *The World According To Noddy* (2014) – he emphasised the impact of Slade's new success, recalling a 20-November-1971 gig at the Starlight Ballroom in Boston, Lincolnshire:

> The realisation that I may be *famous*, hit me hard ... We'd been gigging practically every night since 1966, going down a storm in towns and cities the length and breadth of country. But that night in Boston was like nothing we had ever experienced before ... Hands were reaching out and grabbing me, clutching at my legs. Being pulled back and forth, trying to stay upright on platform shoes, and singing into the microphone while still playing guitar, became impossible. I lost my balance, toppled back, banged my head on a cymbal and hit the carpeted stage hard.

Slade had finally made it and, as Holder alludes to above, the lives of the four band members would be very different from then on. In a 2018 interview with the author, the more self-effacing Lea shared his own thoughts on sudden success and fame:

> The idea of fame is very nice. You think that's what you want, but when it comes – well, it took me all of a couple of weeks to think, 'Hang on, I haven't got a life here'. You couldn't go anywhere. You couldn't do anything. So a lot of people want that and they want that attention, whereas, with me, I wanted to go back to how I was before going on television.

Boston was just one of around 140 gigs the band played in 1971. After a short break from May to June, they gigged almost constantly until December. Three October gigs were played in front of a live audience at Command Studios in London's Piccadilly, and were to have lasting importance for Slade's career. This was where they recorded their first live album, which was released the following year.

Five years of hard slog had finally paid off, and 1971 had seen Slade's breakthrough. They ended the year by featuring on one of two Christmas editions of *Top Of The Pops*. Broadcast on 27 December, they played 'Coz I Luv You', appearing alongside a number of other chart-toppers from that year, like T. Rex and Rod Stewart. But 1972 would take the band into stratospheric levels of success.

Chapter Four: 1972 – Slaying Them Alive

The huge success that Slade saw in late-1971, would continue into 1972 when they would score four top five hits – including two more number ones – and two top-selling albums. It would also be the year that glam rock really took off, and by the end of the year, a host of other artists would have joined T. Rex and Slade with stomping singles, enormous silver platforms and copious amounts of glitter.

Look Wot You Dun single
Personnel:
Noddy Holder: lead vocals, rhythm guitar
Dave Hill: lead guitar, backing vocals
Jim Lea: bass, piano, backing vocals
Don Powell: drums, vocal effects
Studio: Olympic, London, 1971
Producer: Chas Chandler
Release date: UK: January 1972
Chart places: UK: 4, US: -

'Look Wot You Dun' (Holder, Lea, Powell) b/w **'Candidate'** (Lea, Powell)
Slade's first single of the year was a song that initially emerged from the Lea/Powell pairing. Powell recalled in his biography: 'I wrote the lyrics to that one. But I couldn't really finish it, so Nod came up with the chorus'. As the person responsible for finishing the song, Holder expressed some unhappiness with 'Look Wot You Dun' in his autobiography: 'We knew at the time it wasn't one of our best records, but we had to put something out straight away. We couldn't go back to releasing covers, and 'Look Wot You Dun' was the best we could come up with at short notice'. Though the song isn't wild and raucous like 'Get Down And Get With It', it still has that trademark stomp and an irresistibly catchy chorus. Pounding piano and Powell's zany heavy breathing help make it distinct.

The B-side 'Candidate' by Lea and Powell was an unusually political song for the band. With a world-weary lyric about unscrupulous politicians making electoral promises they have little intention of keeping, the track nicely captured the mood of the early-1970s as previous post-war political certainties begin to evaporate:

What we really want is some way to adjust
All the values that we have been left to trust
I just can't believe
They're real, very real
Far from real

With its thudding bass line and neat riff, 'Candidate' is a continuation of the sophisticated hard rock the band pursued on *Play It Loud*, and, in spite of the trademark handclaps, it's a world away from the glam raunch of their big singles.

Praising its 'high drama' and 'menacing beat', *NME*'s Chris Welch predicted 'Look Wot You Dun' would be another smash. But it wasn't quite the smash its predecessor was. Like 'Coz I Luv You', 'Look Wot You Dun' entered the UK charts in the mid-20s, reaching the top ten the following week. Unlike its predecessor, it peaked no higher than four. It reached number two in the Netherlands, six in Ireland and reached the top 20 in Belgium and Germany. It was still a huge achievement, but no match for the success that came before it, or indeed immediately after. Nevertheless, it was becoming more and more obvious that Slade were going to be around for some time. In addition to the inevitable *Top Of The Pops* appearances, there were TV slots on chart shows in Switzerland, the Netherlands and France, and there was no shortage of press coverage, either.

In a February-1972 *Times* article, music critic Richard Williams welcomed the new musical approach that the likes of Bolan and Slade represented: 'After a couple of years devoted to worthy but dull earnestness, rock and roll is back where it belongs – in the streets, in the sweaty ballroom, the paperboy's whistle'. At this stage, glam rock was still pretty much the two acts, albeit two hugely popular ones. There were, of course, obvious differences between Slade and T. Rex. In spite of both bands sharing a penchant for outrageously-colourful clobber, and Hill taking Bolan's lead and dabbing on a bit of facial glitter, the down-to-earth nature of Slade and their ribald Black-Country humour, made for a contrast with the far-more-effete Bolan and his love of whimsical, mystical narratives. In *Who's Crazee Now?,* Holder examines the difference between the two bands:

Bolan was a little skinny bloke with corkscrew hair; very sweet and unassuming. I think we liked each other. At least, I know we all liked him. He was always nice and polite when we met, but it was obvious that he was quite frightened of us. He was very careful what he said to us. He came from a completely different background, and you could tell he thought we were a bunch of yobbos from up north.

In *Glam Rock: Music In Sound And Vision,* Simon Phillo also compared Slade to Bolan, concluding about the former: 'Never remotely androgynous, the band did, however, appreciate the value of putting on a show'. One of the *Slade Fan Club* newsletters that year even gave tips on how to look like Dave Hill: 'The first step is to buy a tube of glitter. But be warned, it will cost you 4p, so check your finances'.

While T. Rex and Slade were still the dominant acts in what became known as glam rock, they did not have it all to themselves for very long. 1972 was the year glam really took off. After the more-melodic art rock of *Hunky Dory*, Bowie fully embraced glam, enjoying success with the 'Starman' single and its album *The Rise And Fall of Ziggy Stardust And The Spiders From Mars*. Following several lightweight bubblegum hits, The Sweet also switched to a more overt glam sound and image with 'Wig-Wam Bam' - the first single where they were allowed to play as well as sing. Meanwhile, the newly-renamed Gary Glitter also enjoyed his first hit that year with 'Rock And Roll (Parts 1 & 2)'. For Bolan and T. Rex, the competition led to a gradual decline in chart fortunes over the coming years. But throughout the highpoint of the glam era during 1972-1974, Slade came to dominate and outsell all of their contemporaries.

One of the reasons put forward for the rise of glam in this period was the growing popularity of colour television. Colour first came to UK TV screens via BBC2 in 1967, followed by BBC1 and ITV in 1969. According to statistics from the National Science and Media Museum, in March 1969, there were barely 100,000 colour TV sets in the UK. This doubled to 200,000 by 1970. But by 1972, there were 1,600,000 in operation. Though middle-aged parents who were buying or renting the new sets may have had little interest in *Top Of The Pops* and its ilk, their teenage offspring certainly did. Hill says in his book: 'If ever a band was made for colour television, it was us!'. Certainly, Slade made many TV appearances in 1972, when the world was first introduced to Holder's mirrored top hat and an ever-more-outrageous selection of silver costumes from the glitter-festooned Hill.

Now that the band had a handful of hits behind them, the venues and the crowds were starting to get bigger, too. Slade's 1972 tour schedule was utterly relentless. Beginning at Cambridge's Corn Exchange on January 1, they toured the UK continually until April. Fan, John Parton, was at Wolverhampton Civic Hall on 6 March 1972 for his first ever gig: 'I was twelve years old. I got my seat down at the front but did not really know what to expect. Slade came on, the crowd rushed forward and it was just an unbelievable experience for a twelve year old.' Then there were a handful of gigs in Belgium, and it was back to the UK, before a tour of Holland in late April and early May. There was then a short UK tour where they were supported by Status Quo. The rest of the year carried on in a similar vein. Mainly, the band were headlining, but there were also some festivals and one-off package gigs. Tony Stewart of *NME* caught Slade at the Locarno Club in Coventry on 3 February 1972, when the band shared a bill with Chuck Berry, Billy Preston and the Roy Young Band. Stewart wrote: 'As usual, they worked hard at stirring the audience up, with Noddy Holder telling them to stand up and let rip. His course remarks shook a few people off their rumps, and I must admit to being an ardent fan of the band after such a showy and exuberant set.'

Of far greater significance was the Great Western Express Festival in Bardney, Lincolnshire, on 28 May. On a bill packed with more-serious album-orientated acts, many in the audience deemed Slade's presence to be an unwelcome teenybop incursion. In their respective autobiographies, Hill, Holder and Powell recounted how Slade were booed when they first went onstage but within minutes had won over the rock crowd. Slade fan Bryan Parker who was at the festival takes up the story: 'After three days of very indifferent weather, the band came on to face the largely hippy crowd, and promptly blew the place apart. The audience went wild. They saved the day for many of us'. *Sounds* reviewer Ray Telford emphasised the point: 'On paper, Slade looked dreadfully out of place among all the heavies at Lincoln. But on stage, they more than held their own, and as I say, there must now be considerably more Slade aficionados than ever before'.

Even if fans were not lucky enough to see Slade live for themselves, they could now purchase the band's live album, which came out that Spring.

Slade Alive! album (1972)

Personnel:
Noddy Holder: lead vocals, rhythm guitar
Dave Hill: lead guitar, backing vocals

Jim Lea: bass, backing vocals
Don Powell: drums
Studios: Command, London; Mixed at Olympic, London, 1971
Producer: Chas Chandler
Release date: UK: March 1972
Chart places: UK: 2, US: 158
Running time: 39:00
Tracklisting: Side One: 1. 'Hear Me Calling' (Lee), 2. 'In Like A Shot From My Gun' (Holder, Lea, Powell – credited on the album as 'Slade'), 3. 'Darling Be Home Soon' (Sebastian), 4. 'Know Who You Are' (Holder, Lea, Hill. Powell – credited on the album as 'Slade')
Side Two: 1. 'Keep On Rocking' (Holder, Lea, Hill, Powell – credited on the album as 'Slade'), 2. 'Get Down And Get With It' (Marchan), 3. 'Born To Be Wild' (Bonfire)

> It was a bit of a retro album, very much more the way we'd been prior to having hits, and again Chas's timing was spot on. 12 months before, we'd only been known as a live band, but after three hits we suddenly had fans who didn't know that side of us.
> (Dave Hill, *So Here It Is: The Autobiography*, 2017)

In making the live album, Slade played three consecutive nights in October 1971 in front of an audience at Command Studios, though all of the album came from the second night. Situated at 201 Piccadilly in London's West End, the BBC had used it as a broadcasting space for decades, before selling it off as surplus to requirements. It was then turned into a three-studio complex and renamed Command. Studio one – previously used for light entertainment shows with a studio audience – was the ideal location for the live recording, as it could comfortably accommodate several hundred fans each night.

Slade Alive! came in a gatefold sleeve with what became an iconic cover showing the band on stage, silhouetted in black on a red background. If the previous album's sepia cover showed a band not quite sure of their musical identity, *Slade Alive!* screamed out loud what this band was all about. The initial idea was to get a fan to design the cover (via a competition in *The Sun*), but in the end, the competition winner's artwork – an irreverent cartoon of a naked wizard and a giant dog – appeared on the inside sleeve. However, in a handful of countries (notably France, Israel and Italy), the cartoon was on the front cover.

Including only one of Slade's recent hits, *Slade Alive!* showcases a side of the band that many of the newer fans were less familiar with. Eschewing the two most recent hit singles, the album contains some thrilling cover versions – including the album opener: an energetic version of Alvin Lee's 'Hear Me Calling', from the Ten Years After album, *Stonedhenge*. One of only three original Slade songs on the album, 'In Like A Shot From My Gun' is a slice of hard rock in the style of *Play It Loud*, though the song never appeared on a studio album.

Slade transform the gentle folk-pop of The Lovin' Spoonful's 'Darling Be Home Soon' into an emotive, soulful *tour de force*, with a spine-tingling Holder vocal and haunting lead guitar from Hill as the band build to a dramatic crescendo. 'Know Who You Are' – the Slade song that began life as the instrumental 'Genesis' – gets another outing here; this live rendition becoming the definitive version. The following track, 'Keep On Rockin'' – cheekily credited as a band composition – is basically recycled 1950s rock-and-roll riffs, with a hefty chunk of the lyric from Little Richard's 'Tutti Frutti'. But it's a fun, raucous bit of live rock and roll.

A further two covers close the album – the first is the familiar 'Get Down And Get With It'. If people thought that the single brought some good-time, old-style rock and roll raunch to modern pop music a year previously, the incendiary live version takes it to a whole new level with Holder's voice almost blowing the roof off the studio. Then they launch into 'Born To Be Wild' - their regular set closer at the time. The energy levels are palpably higher than the studio version on the Ambrose Slade album, ending with a glorious over-the-top jam replete with sirens and a crazed guitar solo from Hill.

Not only does the album showcase Holder as an incredibly powerful vocalist, and the band as talented and versatile musicians, it perfectly captures their ability to engage a crowd, and it is full of characteristically-irreverent banter – from Holder 'getting his key' before roaring out the opening line of 'Get Down And Get With It', to a misplaced burp during one of the quiet sections of 'Darling Be Home Soon'.

NME's Roy Carr was impressed with the album: 'Slade's new album is overtly raucous, vulgar, brash, ribald, flashy, raw and blatantly unsubtle. In other words, it has all the basic ingredients that go to make up a good-old ballsy album of degenerate rock 'n' roll'. The *Record Mirror* review noted, 'It's a rockin' album, and the excitement of the group and crowd has been captured well'. In the US, *Phonograph Record*'s Greg Shaw was similarly impressed: 'This is one of the best live albums I've ever heard. I think Slade's the band that's gonna do it. They're getting the same phenomenal coverage in the British press that T. Rex and David Bowie got when they began to break loose. And if the pattern holds, we can expect to hear a lot more from them'. *Rolling Stone'*s Jon Tiven praised *Slade Alive!* as 'a true recreation of concert visceral release', and perhaps a little over-confidently, predicted, 'Having taken England quite by storm, Noddy and James and Donald and David are certain to do the same in America'.

The enthusiasm of the music press certainly matched sales in the UK, where the album went to number two and spent 57 weeks in the top 50. But in the US – where the album scraped in at 158 – there were clear signs that the American public weren't taking to Slade quite so easily. Nevertheless, Slade and Chandler could content themselves with a number one in Australia, and top 20 placings in Austria and Norway.

The month *Slade Alive!* came out, the compilation *Coz I Luv You* was released in a number of European countries, Australia and (with a different title) Argentina. There were some tracklist variations, but the compilations were culled from *Play It Loud* and various singles. UK fans would have to wait until September 1973 for the definitive Slade compilation *Sladest*. But they did not have to wait long for a new single.

Take Me Bak 'Ome single

Personnel:
Noddy Holder: lead vocals, rhythm guitar
Dave Hill: lead guitar, backing vocals
Jim Lea: bass, backing vocals
Don Powell: drums
Studio: Olympic, London, 1972
Producer: Chas Chandler
Release date: UK: May 1972
Chart places: UK: 1, US: 97

'Take Me Bak 'Ome' (Holder, Lea) b/w 'Wonderin' Y' (Lea, Powell)
If 'Look Wot You Dun' was quirky and slightly left-field, then its follow-up 'Take Me Bak 'Ome' was yobbish, rowdy, raucous Slade at its very best – the first of a hat-trick of classic, era-defining singles from the band that year – 'Lots of aggro fuzz, menacing handclaps and virile vocals', as *NME'*s Chris Welch put it, correctly predicting another 'boot-stomping chart hit'.

In sharp contrast, the B-side 'Wonderin' Y' was a beautiful melodic ballad with a poignant lyric. Powell's stint as one of the main lyricists would soon come to an end, but songs like this make you wish he had carried on just a little longer.

Though 'Take Me Bak 'Ome' reached number one, Slade were still some way from the straight-in-at-number-one routine they were to perfect the following year. Instead, the single entered at 25 in the first week of June, went to 14 the following week, spent a week at number three, then a week at two, before finally reaching number one. It went top five in Ireland and the Netherlands, top ten in South Africa and Germany, top 20 in Australia and Belgium, and sneaked up to 97 in the US. This was the band's first – albeit minor – taste of US chart success. There was the usual round of *Top Of The Pops* appearances, *Lift Off With Ayshea*, and *2 Gs And The Pop People* featuring an amusing sequence of female dancers dressed like each Slade member and dancing alongside their respective doppelganger.

Though it did not contain their then-current hit, Slade appeared live on a Granada TV programme called *Set Of Six*, broadcast on 13 June 1972. The full broadcast eventually found its way onto the 2005 DVD *The Very Best Of Slade*. With the band performing an explosive set consisting of 'Hear Me Calling', Look Wot You Dun', Darling Be Home Soon', 'Coz I Luv You', 'Get Down And Get With It' and 'Born To Be Wild', it's very much a visual companion to *Slade Alive!*, and is well worth seeking out.

Mama Weer All Crazee Now single

Personnel:
Noddy Holder: lead vocals, rhythm guitar
Dave Hill: lead guitar, backing vocals
Jim Lea: bass, backing vocals
Don Powell: drums
Studio: Olympic, London, 1972
Producer: Chas Chandler
Release date: UK: August 1972
Chart places: UK: 1, US: 76

'Mama Weer All Crazee Now' (Holder, Lea) b/w **'Man Who Speaks Evil'** (Lea, Powell)
By now, Holder and Lea had their formula for writing smash singles down to a tee, and developed their own unique take on the glam phenomenon.

The songs were wild, raucous and unrelenting, with lyrics about having the time of your life – not for them the esoteric, art-school cool or otherworldly themes that preoccupied others working within the glam sphere. 'Mama Weer All Crazee Now' was another slice of Slade perfection. In his autobiography, Holder recounted how the lyric idea came after surveying the havoc that crazed fans wreaked on Wembley Arena after a gig. With the chorus conceived as 'My my, we're all crazy now', Chandler somehow misheard it and thought they were singing 'Mama'. Realising the misheard title was far better – even if the meaning became slightly more opaque – the song was renamed and quickly recorded.

Predicting it would be another number one, *NME*'s Danny Holloway wrote, 'From the fuzzed-out guitar intro to the rockin', stompin' chorus, through to the crowd singing along at the end, Slade personify the excitement of the current 45 market'.

'Man Who Speaks Evil' had the distinction of being the final Lea/Powell B-side. Though Powell wasn't discouraged from writing once the Holder/Lea partnership was firmly established, he was happy to take a back seat: 'Noddy Holder and Jim Lea started writing, and they were doing it like that and they were coming out with the hits, and it was so easy for them. So I just let them carry on with it'.

Entering the charts at number two on 2 September, with the band almost perfecting the knack of going straight in at number one but not quite, the single rose to the top position the following week. Here it would spend three weeks, with the band chalking up another run of *Top Of The Pops* appearances. The single would make number one in Ireland, number three in Norway, number five in Switzerland, number six in Austria and Germany and number seven in the Netherlands, as well as Top Twenty in Australia, Belgium and Finland. Although nowhere near on a par with their success in Europe, the single also made it to 76 in the US *Billboard* Hot 100.

Following the May tour with Status Quo, Slade toured Europe throughout the summer. *NME*'s Graham Punter caught the madness that was, by now, a typical Slade concert - at Dunstable on 24 June: 'Even at its height, Beatlemania would've been hard-pressed to produce scenes such as prevailed at the California, Dunstable, on Saturday night. Guys screamed for air, and girls fainted, as Slade rocked and socked it to a capacity audience behind locked doors'.

In September, the band embarked on their first US tour, beginning in Sacramento on the 2nd, and finishing in Detroit on the 25th September

– with a brief trip to Belgium for a festival halfway through. The band were mainly supporting Humble Pie. Greg Shaw of *Phonograph Record* interviewed Holder at the time:

> It's good first comin' to America, because of all this sort of adulation we get in Europe ... We've got to start all over again in America, playin' the bottom of the bill, gettin' the audience to know the songs and that. It's just like startin' all over again. It's makin' us better for it ... We're a workin'-class band, workin'-class kids. Bolan has sort of a star quality on stage and he's not touchable. With us, the audience is part of the band. The music is just 50% of Slade. The dressing up and the humour and the audience involvement is the other 50%. That's the difference.

After returning from the US in September, Slade then embarked on a short European tour during October of 1972. Fan Heather Blandford was at one of the German dates:

> I first saw Slade on 26 October 1972 at the Deutschlandhalle in Berlin, where my father was stationed at the time. 'Mama Weer All Crazee Now' had been released the month before, and the whole place erupted when they played it. The whole concert was brilliant. I remember the massive stack of loudspeakers, and the sound coming out of them was out of this world. We all came away hooked.

Gudbuy T' Jane single

Personnel:
Noddy Holder: lead vocals, rhythm guitar
Dave Hill: lead guitar, backing vocals
Jim Lea: bass, backing vocals
Don Powell: drums
Studio: Olympic, London, 1972
Producer: Chas Chandler
Release date: UK: November 1972
Chart places: UK: 2, US: 68

'Gudbuy T' Jane' (Holder, Lea) b/w **'I Won't Let It 'Appen Again'** (Lea)
'Gudbuy T' Jane' came to Lea on a day off from the US tour. The Jane in question was a glamorous young co-host of a US chat show that the

band had appeared on. Jane was proud of what she called her "40s trip boots', but mislaid them on the day Slade arrived for filming, causing much drama, to the amusement of the band. Lea began writing the song, using the melody from an earlier song he had never completed. Holder finished the lyric and changed Lea's chorus line to 'Hello to Jane'. Thankfully, he was outvoted by Chandler and the rest of the band. When it came to recording it, when there was some remaining time at the end of a session, Chandler had asked them if they had any other material to hand. Holder recalled in his book: 'We played it to Chas, and he loved it. He said, 'Get this down on tape now. You've got 30 minutes'. The song was perfected over the coming days, and with its distinctive drum intro, neat riff and sing-along chorus, Slade had turned out another classic.

Lea wrote the B-side 'I Won't Let It Happen Again' alone, and – unusually for a Slade B-side – it was included on the coming album *Slayed?*.

NME reviewer Chris Welch enjoyed the guitar and bass patterns and praised Holder's 'immensely powerful voice', predicting that: 'The band seem set for a further year of hits, judging from the exuberant confidence their music enjoys'. While the single garnered the band a run of *Top Of The Pops* appearances (three via a promotional video, and one studio performance), unlike its predecessor, it did not reach number one. Entering the UK charts at number eight in the final week of November, three weeks later it would peak at number two but was kept off the top slot by Chuck Berry's 'My Ding-A-Ling'. Ireland also sent it to number two and it would make the Top Five in Belgium, Germany, the Netherlands and Switzerland with a slew of Top Twenty positions elsewhere. Over in the US, the single crept up to number 68 in the *Billboard* Hot 100. This would be the band's highest-ranking US chart position until 'My Oh My' and 'Run Run Away' were released over a decade later.

In November 1972, Slade set out on a 23-date UK tour, commencing at Newcastle City Hall on 3 November, concluding at Bristol's Colston Hall on 5 December. With Thin Lizzy as the main support act, the tour was also noteworthy for an opening slot from the recently-enlisted Mickie Most and RAK protégé Suzi Quatro. *NME*'s Julie Webb was at Newcastle City Hall on the first night: 'Kicking off with 'Hear Me Calling', the audience went stomping, clapping and leaping into action. Arms swayed, waved and gesticulated – strictly observing whatever Holder and the rest of Slade would have them do. It's almost terrifying to watch the power of the band over an audience'.

Slayed? album (1972)
Personnel:
Noddy Holder: lead vocals, rhythm guitar
Dave Hill: lead guitar, backing vocals
Jim Lea: bass, backing vocals
Don Powell: drums
Studio: Olympic, London, 1972
Producer: Chas Chandler
Release date: UK: December 1972
Chart places: UK: 1, US: 69
Running time: 34:30

> It was a defining record for us – not least because of the sleeve, which has become iconic for us.
> (Dave Hill, *So Here It Is: The Autobiography*, 2017)

Following the phenomenally successful live album, Slade released their second album of the year and their third studio album while 'Gudbuy T' Jane' was still working its way up the charts. If *Beginnings* was their US-influenced psychedelic album, *Play It Loud* their progressive hard rock album, and *Slade Alive!* a representation of their live act, then *Slayed?* was most definitely more representative of the sound that was giving them a consistent run of hit singles. Though only two of the hits appear here, the trademark Slade stomp carries across the whole album. *Slayed?* eventually earned a place in Robert Dimery's encyclopaedic *1,001 Albums You Must Hear Before You Die* (2005), with reviewer Ross Fortune praising the album as 'a great hefty wodge of pure, prime, shouty and sing-along period pop'.

The cover is almost as iconic as the album itself – including a shirtless Hill, and the band with their thumbs outstretched and their fists pointing to the camera and spelling out the word 'S-L-A-D-E'.

'How D'You Ride' (Holder, Lea)
With its big intro, big riff and big sound, 'How D'You Ride' pretty much sets the template for the rest of *Slayed?*. In his biography *Look Wot I Dun*, Powell states that the song was in contention to be a single at one point.

'The Whole World's Goin' Crazee' (Holder)
Wild, raucous and wonderfully over-the-top, this track can be seen as
a companion of sorts to 'Mama Weer All Crazee Now', but written from
the perspective of the band rather than the audience. This is the album's
sole Holder song.

'Look At Last Nite' (Holder, Lea)
A slow, pounding number, very much in the spirit of 'Coz I Luv You'
and 'Look Wot You Dun', 'Look At Last Nite' brings a welcome change
of pace. But even so, the band still give it their all with a powerful
trademark stomp. The lyric deals with the downside of fame and the
fickle celebrity culture.

'I Won't Let It 'Appen Agen' (Lea)
This is the album's sole Lea offering, which was also the B-side of
'Gudbuy T' Jane'. A mid-tempo song with an effective machine-gun bass
part, it is written from the standpoint of a regretful lover asking for a
second chance.

'Move Over' (Janis Joplin)
This first of the album's covers originally appeared on Janis Joplin's
Pearl. Slade had recorded a version of it for a BBC radio session
broadcast in May 1972, and Joplin was the perfect female vocalist for
them to cover.

   You can hear from that session (available on *Slade Live At The BBC*
(Salvo, 2009)) why it was ideal material, and the band suitably *Sladify*
it to make it their own. Polydor released it as a single in Japan, b/w 'Let
the Good Times Roll/Feel So Fine'.

'Gudbuy T' Jane' (Holder, Lea)
The first of the two recent hit singles, covered earlier in the chapter.

'Gudbuy Gudbuy' (Holder, Lea)
Although similarly titled to the fun, irreverent hit single that precedes it,
this is a moody breakup song, with an unrelenting, heavy bass line and
a superb guitar solo.

'Mama Weer All Crazee Now' (Holder, Lea)
The second of the recent hit singles, covered earlier in the chapter.

'I Don' Mind' (Holder, Lea)

A slow, brooding song with a menacing lyric hinting at cruelty and even violence, this is far from being a good-time party anthem. But the band play great, even if the words leave you with a bit of a chill.

'Let The Good Times Roll/Feel So Fine' (Lee)

Originally recorded in 1956 by the duo Shirley and Lee, Chandler would have been very familiar with this song, as he recorded it himself with The Animals for their second album. While The Animals went for a jaunty, lighthearted pastiche, Slade totally transform the song, with an unrelenting powerhouse rhythm and Holder yelling the vocals, to truly make it their own. It segues seamlessly into another Shirley and Lee song, 'Feel So Good' (here titled 'Feel So Fine'). The 'N Betweens had also recorded the song for their 1965 EP. As with the early-1960s beat boom, glam rock was never far away from its traditional rock-and-roll/ R&B heritage.

Polydor released it as a single in the US, b/w 'I Don' Mind'.

Reviewing *Slayed?* for *Sounds*, Billy Walker wrote: '*Slayed?* has everything you'd expect – very few surprises, but music that'll get you up and jumpin' if you're within a four-to-74-year-old age group'. In *Let It Rock*, Charlie Gillett wrote: 'There's only one major flaw with Slade at the moment, which is in the construction of their songs. There's no bridge; no place where the verse pattern changes to give relief. So they all seem to crash along for longer than necessary (to a non-dancing listener anyway). Otherwise, this is an impressively-strong record considering only two tracks are established singles'.

In the US, *Creem*'s Greg Shaw dished out some backhanded compliments: 'Their music is unimaginative, formulaic and monotonous, and it teaches us nothing. But does it ever sound good! Heavy beat, pounding rhythm, lyrics about drinking, dancing or nothing at all ... The fact that Slade currently makes some of the very best records a rock-&-roll fan could desire is all that matters'. Acknowledging that Slade had not had an easy ride in the US thus far, *Rolling Stone*'s Lenny Kaye predicted a tad over-optimistically that *Slayed?* should 'turn all that around, and fast', arguing, 'It is both the group's best and most commercially-cohesive effort to date'.

Entering the UK charts at number five on 9 December, by mid-January, it had risen to number one, a pattern that would be repeated with the two subsequent albums. Moreover, *Slayed?* made number one in Australia, too, and was top ten in Austria, France, Germany, the Netherlands and Norway. It was often quite unusual for successful singles acts to have similar album-chart success. T. Rex achieved it, but Sweet and Suzi Quatro were not nearly so lucky. But it merely demonstrated how huge Slade had become by the end of 1972. Could they get any bigger in 1973? Of course they could.

Chapter Five: 1973 – Feeling The Noize

1973 was destined to be glam's *annus mirabilis*. In that year, glam rock acts including The Sweet, Wizzard, Suzi Quatro and Gary Glitter would occupy the UK top spot for an incredible 28 weeks out of 52. Slade would be a huge part of this success, of course, chalking up three number ones and a number two that year. But it would also be a year of tragedy, and uncertainty over Slade's future. The band would soon pick up the pieces, however, and would end the year with the release of a Christmas single, which the band's name would forever become almost synonymous with.

Slade started the year by performing a special gig at the London Palladium, as part of the Fanfare For Europe concert series to mark the start of the UK's forty-seven-year membership of the EEC (later EU). Reviewing the concert for *NME*, James Johnson wrote: 'It would be hard to ignore Jim Lea's tremendous bass-playing, or Noddy Holder's voice: the kind that knocks your head back. On Sunday, it sounded as if it could be heard halfway down Oxford Street'.

Later in January, the band headed to New Zealand and Australia for their first tour there, starting in Hamilton, New Zealand, taking in Sydney, Brisbane, Adelaide, Melbourne, and back to Sydney for a show at the 5,000-capacity Hordern Pavilion. Helen Crowe of *The Herald* reviewed the 4-February Melbourne Showgrounds concert: 'Although exciting and high powered, Slade's numbers were predictable. The rasping Noddy even ad-libbed in the same places as he does in the three Slade albums. It was disappointing; there was no new material. 'Keep On Rocking', 'Take Me Bak 'Ome, 'Gudbuy T' Jane' and, of course, 'Get Down And Get With It', were met with raucous rocking, stomping and clapping from the crowd'. Then it was back to the UK for the release of Slade's fastest-selling single yet.

Cum On Feel The Noize single
Personnel:
Noddy Holder: lead vocals, rhythm guitar
Dave Hill: lead guitar, backing vocals
Jim Lea: bass, backing vocals
Don Powell: drums
Studio: Olympic, London, 1973
Producer: Chas Chandler

Release date: UK: February 1973
Chart places: UK: 1, US: 98

'Cum On Feel The Noize' (Holder, Lea) b/w **'I'm Mee, I'm Now And That's Orl'** (Holder, Lea)
In terms of an anthem that captured the wild, frenetic and crazy buzz of Slade live, it was going to be difficult to top 'Mama Weer All Crazee Now'. But with 'Cum On Feel The Noize', they pulled it off magnificently. If it had not been for a certain Christmas record, 'Cum On Feel The Noize' was always destined to be Slade's best-known and best-loved song. Holder said in his book: 'Even before the single came out, we knew it was going to be a monster hit'.

The non-album B-side 'I'm Mee, I'm Now And That's Orl' is a superb slice of brooding heavy rock, its slower tempo and more feet-on-the-ground down-to-earth lyric contrasting nicely with the A-side.

Sounds described the single as a 'rousing, raucous, rocker that follows its predecessors with an instantly recognisable sound'. In terms of marketing, nothing was going to be left to chance. Chandler and Polydor devised a plan to ensure the single went straight to number one. Their strategy was to use pre-publicity to maximise advance orders, and ensured stacks of the single were distributed to shops in the week running up to the release date, so it was available to buy as soon as it came out.

'Cum On Feel The Noize' was previewed on *Top Of The Pops* the evening before its 23 February release date. The performance has Hill appearing in his famous 'metal nun' outfit, a black floor-length coat and silver headdress, each festooned in mirrors. Hill's outfits were getting more outrageous with every appearance. Keith Altham in the *NME* that week: 'He comes on stage with Slade like an overdecorated, perambulating Christmas tree, smothered in silver stars, gold and glitter from head to toe. But somehow, he never minces into the realm of the camp.' Hill reflected in the same article: 'I made up my mind some time ago that I really just wanted to help focus attention on the band, and I've worked at it and exaggerated my own style. I've always been a bit flash, and all I had to do was get up enough nerve to go on stage and be as outrageous as I felt'.

The combination of a brilliant song from the UK's biggest band at the time and a shrewd marketing plan, sent the single straight to number one the week it was released – the first time this had happened since

The Beatles released 'Get Back' in 1969. Debuting in the UK at number one, the single spent four weeks occupying the top slot, as well as making the Top Twenty in Australia, Austria, Belgium, Finland, France, Germany, the Netherlands and Switzerland; and reaching number one in Ireland, too.

The release of 'Cum On Feel The Noize' was timed to coincide with a one-off gig at Manchester's 3,000-capacity Hardrock Concert Theatre on 27 February 1973, when the band shared a bill with Fairport Convention and Beck, Bogert & Appice. Slade fan Alan Whitney was there:

> My first gig was Slade at Hardrock Feb '73, the day 'Cum On Feel The Noize' charted at number 1! I took my sister. We were five rows from the stage; never been so hot or heard anything as loud. Nod at the fifth song into the set: 'We had a bit of news today'. Cue crowd mayhem. Then Slade played 'Cum On Feel The Noize' just like *Top Of The Pops*, right in front of us fans all balanced carefully on the seats! Slade were amazing. The crowd went crazy. My ears took three days to recover.

Following some mainland Europe dates that spring, and two shows at Wembley's Empire Pool (subsequently renamed Wembley Arena), Slade set out on their second US tour. Starting in Warren, Ohio, on 19 April – taking in the likes of New York City, Boston, Chicago, Cleveland, San Francisco and Milwaukee, with a handful of dates in Canada – the band crisscrossed North America, supporting acts like Johnny Winter, Humble Pie and The Eagles. Lillian Roxon of the *New York Sunday News* was at New York's Academy of Music for the tour's second night:

> When Slade finally came on, the entire audience seemed asleep. Their exhortation to 'Get down and get with it' was greeted with blank stares. It was an awful audience to play to, and Slade knew it. But within 20 minutes, people were slowly getting up on their feet. Slowly and self-consciously, they began stamping and waving their arms until whole rows – and then whole sections – were up. True, it was a bit late, and Noddy Holder – who wants the audience to be his in the first ten seconds – grumbled a bit. But I thought it was a miracle. In the end, the cheers were deafening. Slade had done it again.

Holder's unique approach to audience participation, and the consequent culture shock for the more laid-back US audiences the band encountered, became something of a recurring theme of reviewers on that tour. *Phonograph Record*'s Ken Barnes deemed the show at Santa Monica Civic Center a major letdown:

> Nearly every song was preceded, followed and internally interrupted by a time-consuming and corrosive Noddy Holder ultimatum to get off our butts, get on top of our seats and get down with it in terms of vocal participation. If Slade could take that hint, stop trying to harangue the crowd into an artificial state of excitement, and instead get up there and power through those incredible singles and some of their dynamite LP cuts, they could conquer America in no time.

At the same gig, *Music World*'s Richard Cromelin wrote:

> It's a pity ... that a band that can make such incredible singles as 'Gudbye T'Jane' and 'Mama, Weer All Crazy Now' (not to mention spell as charmingly as they do), must approach its audience as a wild horse to be brutally tamed, when the music alone is all the inducement we need to conduct ourselves as a proper rock-'n'-roll crowd. If dear Noddy didn't spend five minutes between each song telling us to clap along and get out of our seats, we would still have been clapping and standing, instead of listening from out in the lobby.

The *NME's* Keith Altham was sent to cover the US tour. In his article 'Slade in the USA: Will Slade break America or will America break Slade?', he wrote: 'Slade's major problem is to find a younger audience because major rock-concert audiences in America are still elder students going to see more-established bands like Pie, the Stones, Zeppelin, Tull and ELP. And that's not Slade's bag'. Interviewed for the article, Holder seemed to agree: 'We'd like a younger crowd. But with the state of things in America, I think the parents are keeping the kids at home. We'll get to them, but it'll take time'. But whatever US audiences felt about Slade in 1973, it was a different matter back in the UK. At the end of May, Slade were back home for another sold-out tour and the release of another smash single.

Skweeze Me, Pleeze Me single
Personnel:
Noddy Holder: lead vocals, rhythm guitar
Dave Hill: lead guitar, backing vocals

Jim Lea: bass, backing vocals, violin (B-side)
Don Powell: drums
Studio: Olympic, London, 1973
Producer: Chas Chandler
Release date: UK: June 1973
Chart places: UK: 1, US: –

'Skweeze Me, Pleeze Me' (Holder, Lea) b/w 'Kill 'Em At The Hot Club Tonight' (Holder, Lea)

'Skweeze Me, Pleeze Me' was the last in a run of five fast and furious hard-rocking anthems that began with 'Take Me Bak 'Ome', before the band slowed things down a notch with the likes of 'My Friend Stan'. Though 'Skweeze Me, Pleeze Me' went straight in at number one, it is probably the weakest of the five. Certainly, the melody is catchy but the lyric ('When a girl's meaning yes, she says no') has not stood the test of time and it was a song the band never really got into playing on stage. 'We have come to expect better things from Slade', was the verdict of the *NME's* Chris Welch.

The B-side 'Kill 'Em At The Hot Club Tonight' is a gorgeous, unexpected hot-club-jazz-like number that channels the spirit of Django Reinhardt and Stéphane Grappelli. Holder and Lea were huge fans of the duo, and Lea's violin-playing on the track very much echoes that of Grappelli.

There was a run of three consecutive slots on *Top Of The Pops,* and an appearance on *Lift Off With Ayshea,* where the band also played the B-side. 'Skweeze Me Pleeze Me' spent three weeks at number one in the UK: their second single to go straight to the top spot. The ever-loyal Irish fans also sent it to the top of the charts, and it was a top-five hit in Germany, Norway and Switzerland. Slade were still huge business.

Three weeks prior to the single's release, Slade commenced a UK tour, supported by The Sensational Alex Harvey Band. Starting on 31 May at Green's Playhouse in Glasgow, the tour ran until 15 June, culminating in a one-off concert at the Earls Court Exhibition Centre on 1 July. Slade were booked to be the first rock act to play the venue but were pipped to the post by David Bowie, who performed there that May. Nevertheless, Earls Court was a triumph. Nick Kent enthused in the *NME*: 'The concert was a further testament to Slade's vital importance in what in effect is the total reconstruction of the energies that govern the workings of pure rock-'n'-roll music. If – as was stated before – The Beatles brought *art* back to the masses when such a project seemed impossible, then Slade have brought rock back to the people when it seemed to be going through its final death pangs'.

Chris Charlesworth was equally enthusiastic for *Melody Maker*: 'And so we come to last night: perhaps the final and ultimate climax of the group's career. It would be difficult to imagine Slade – or any group, for that matter – emulating the barrage of fanatical acclaim that Slade won for themselves at Earls Court. It was more of a convention than a concert – a gathering of the converted, that rivalled political assemblies, royal weddings and sporting crowds in both size and fervour'.

Charlesworth's words had a bitter irony given that in the early hours of 4 July – two days after the concert – Powell was involved in a car crash that killed his girlfriend Angela Morris, left Powell unconscious with life-threatening injuries, and put the very future of the band, in doubt. Life carries on in such situations, of course, and in his autobiography, Hill talks about the odd feeling of the crowd dancing along to the band's new single on *Top Of The Pops* while Powell lay in hospital. The band were also contracted to perform two further concerts that month – at the Palace Lido in Douglas, Isle of Man, with Lea's younger brother Frank stepping in on drums. Reviewing the first of the two gigs with Frank Lea, Charlesworth wrote: 'The show itself ran like all Slade shows. The only number they cut out was Janis Joplin's 'Move Over Baby', which features plenty of tricky drum work. The rest of the Slade ingredients were all there – football chants, suggestive remarks, the responding crowd and the deafening noise of Holder's amazingly-powerful voice'.

After a six-week stay in hospital, Powell was discharged, though his injuries left him with severe short-term memory problems and a loss of taste and smell.

Sladest album (1973)
Personnel:
Noddy Holder: lead vocals, rhythm guitar
Dave Hill: lead guitar, backing vocals
Jim Lea: bass, piano, violin, backing vocals
Don Powell: drums
Studio: Olympic, London, 1969-1973
Producer: Chas Chandler
Release date: UK: September 1973
Chart places: UK: 1, US: 129
Running time: 45:47

Tracklisting: Side One: 1. 'Cum On Feel The Noize' (Holder, Lea), 2. 'Look Wot You Dun' (Holder, Lea, Powell), 3. 'Gudbuy T' Jane' (Holder, Lea), 4. 'One Way Hotel' (Holder, Lea, Powell), 5. 'Skweeze Me, Pleeze Me' (Holder, Lea), 6. 'Pouk Hill' (Holder, Lea, Powell), 7. 'The Shape Of Things To Come' (Mann, Weil) Side Two: 1. 'Take Me Bak 'Ome' (Holder, Lea), 2. 'Coz I Luv You' (Holder, Lea), 3. 'Wild Winds Are Blowing' (Saker, Winsley), 4. 'Know Who You Are' (Hill, Holder, Lea, Powell), 5. 'Get Down And Get With It' (Marchan), 6. 'Look At Last Nite' (Holder, Lea), 7. 'Mama Weer All Crazee Now' (Holder, Lea)

> From the moment I heard Slade, I knew they were better musicians than we were.
> **(Chas Chandler in the *Sladest* sleeve notes.)**

Powell's injuries meant that any plans to record a new album were hastily revisited, though it *was* an opportune moment for a Slade compilation. Regardless of Powell's accident, however, the timing of *Sladest* could not have been more perfect. Most of the singles had never appeared on an album, and it was also a good time to introduce the band's glam-era fans to some of the older material. Polydor were rewarded with a number one – in sharp contrast to RCA, who the year before had rush-released *The Sweet's Biggest Hits* before that band were properly in their stride, and that compilation failed to chart at all.

Never the most photogenic of bands in terms of conventional ideas of beauty, Slade were nevertheless given the full soft-focus, teen-pop-idol front-cover shot, courtesy of Gered Mankowitz. The photographer's shot of the band mid-song in full glam regalia in front of a packed crowd at Wolverhampton City Hall, graced the back cover. The original gatefold opened out to reveal an eight-page booklet bearing more band photographs, along with background information on each of the songs.

The *NME*'s Charles Shaar Murray – who was beginning to have a downer on anything glam-related – gave it a grudgingly positive review, calling it an 'excellent' album: 'It gets a bit wearing after too many consecutive plays, mainly due to its non-stop fever pitch. But its sheer ballsiness and power provide enough momentum to tide the listener (that's you, bubeleh) over the dull passages'. In *Let It Rock*, Michael Gray opted for a similar sort of backhanded compliment:

> Personally, I can't stand the kind of community-singing atmosphere that Lester Bangs found so admirable about Slade in concert. I think

it's a grotesque substitute for real communal feeling, and no better when it's elicited by Slade than when it was elicited by that great group of the '30s: Adolph and the Nazis. But on record, bak 'ome, it certainly keeps you awake, which is more than you can say for most 1970s music.

Number one in the UK, *Sladest* was also number one in Finland, and went top-five in Australia, Germany and Norway. With a substantially-revised tracklist (removing the older pre-hit tracks), Reprise released *Sladest* in the US, reaching 129 in *Billboard*. Issued on CD by Salvo in 2011 – as part of their Slade reissues series – it carried a previously-unreleased studio version of 'Hear Me Calling'.

My Friend Stan single
Personnel:
Noddy Holder: lead vocals, rhythm guitar
Dave Hill: lead guitar, backing vocals
Jim Lea: bass, piano, backing vocals
Don Powell: drums
Studio: Olympic, London, 1973
Producer: Chas Chandler
Release date: UK: September 1973
Chart places: UK: 2

'My Friend Stan' (Holder, Lea) b/w **'My Town'** (Holder, Lea)
Though the compilation had come out that autumn, Chandler was keen to release a new single. 'My Friend Stan' came out one week after *Sladest*, and was the first thing Powell recorded following his crash. Not only did it mark the end of the misspelt titles, it also ended the run of blistering, hard-rocking, high-energy singles. A piano-driven track, 'My Friend Stan' can in many ways be seen as a companion to 'Look Wot You Dun'. *Record Mirror* certainly took note of the change of pace, concluding that it was 'in some ways more memorable than the earlier rampagers'. In his autobiography, Holder asserted that the track wasn't originally intended as a single, but was just a stopgap. That may be so, but the single still reached number two in the UK and number one in Ireland, and reached the top five in Germany and Norway. The band made a customary appearance on The *Top Of The Pops* – their first since Powell's accident – for the episode broadcast

on 11 October 1973. But unlike previous singles, this one only got one slot on the show, though there were a string of promo appearances on sundry European pop programmes. The B-side 'My Town' was a far-more-typical slice of classic Slade, and – like the A-side – appeared on the forthcoming album.

Incredibly, Powell was not only back in the studio that autumn, but back on the road, with a rescheduled US tour commencing in New Jersey on 21 September, running through until 21 October. *Melody Maker*'s Chris Charlesworth was there for the tour's final show, where Slade supported the J. Geils Band at Long Beach Arena: 'Slade weren't at their best. Sound problems bit hard into their music. The harsh treble which they use to such good effect, never came over, and Noddy received a series of shocks through the microphone as the set progressed. They're on the way up, but they're not there yet. Whether they will or not is difficult to guess, but there's always been a fierce will to succeed within Slade'. Interviewed for the same article, Holder alluded to the difficulties Powell was still facing: 'He's only just getting back into the stage show as it was before the accident, so we really couldn't try to introduce any new numbers until he was better'.

Despite the setback that summer, the ambition to crack America burned as brightly as ever. Hill told *NME*'s Barbara Charone who was covering the tour: 'The States is the last place we have to make it. Then we'll just do world tours ... God knows when we'll stop. It's a case of getting as big as we possibly can'. Neither Powell nor the other band members were given much time to recover from the tour, as just four days after playing Long Beach Arena, they were off to Belgium for a month-long European tour, ending in Munich on 20 November. But the year was far from over.

Merry Xmas Everybody single

Personnel:
Noddy Holder: lead vocals, rhythm guitar
Dave Hill: lead guitar, backing vocals
Jim Lea: bass, harmonium, acoustic guitar, backing vocals
Don Powell: drums
Studio: The Record Plant, New York, 1973
Producer: Chas Chandler
Release date: UK: December 1973
Chart places: UK: 1, US: –

'Merry Xmas Everybody' (Holder, Lea) b/w **'Don't Blame Me'**
(Holder, Lea)

Over the top, brash, colourful, glittery - glam rock and Christmas seemed
made for each other. Yet glam had been in the ascendancy for two years
before anyone contemplated putting the two together. By the early-
1970s, Christmas singles had been out of fashion for quite some time,
and were more-commonly associated with the saccharine crooning of
Nat King Cole and Bing Crosby than modern pop. 1973 put paid to all
that with two Christmas-themed glam singles making the UK top five that
year: from Wizzard and Slade. But only one was destined to be number
one. From the familiar harmonium in the opening bars to the final 'It's
Christmaaaas!', in the UK, Slade's 'Merry Xmas Everybody' remains one of
the best-known and most popular Christmas records of all time.

We can thank Lea's in-laws for planting the germ of an idea. He told
Uncut in December 2013: 'My mother-in-law the year before had said
why don't we write a song like 'White Christmas': something that can be
played every year'. The chorus of an old song Holder wrote in the 1960s
was resurrected. He wrote most of the lyric and Lea came up with the
melody for the verses.

Unusually for this period, they did not record it at Olympic in London,
but at The Record Plant in New York City. Founded in 1968 by Gary
Kellgren and Chris Stone, the studio was pioneering in providing artists
with a casual, relaxed environment, in contrast to the more clinical
traditional studio setup. (The band were to return there two years later
to record the *Nobody's Fools* album.)

Recorded in a sweltering heatwave in September 1973, Holder told
Uncut some forty years later that he wanted the Christmas song to
convey a mood of optimism. It certainly does that. But at the time of
recording, the band had little clue as to how grim things were going to
get in Britain that particular winter, when Conservative Prime Minister
Ted Heath's increasingly-fractious battle with the miners took a dramatic
turn. Like all public employees at the time, mine workers were suffering
the effects of government-enforced pay caps at a time of hyperinflation
and were pursuing industrial action for higher pay. Given that most of
the country's electricity supply was reliant on coal, regular domestic
power cuts became a fact of life.

'Merry Xmas Everybody' was released on 7 December 1973, and the
band unveiled it on *Top Of The Pops* the night before. Five days later,
Heath announced that in order to conserve coal stocks, the government

Below: Slade pose for photographs in Birmingham City Centre on 25th March 1975. (*Alamy*)

THE GENESIS OF **Slade**

THE VENDORS · STEVE BRETT & THE MAVERICKS
THE 'N BETWEENS

RARE RECORDINGS FROM 1964 TO 1966

Left: Early recordings by The Vendors, Steve Brett & The Mavericks and The 'N Betweens from the mid-1960s were brought together in this 1996 CD compilation. *(TMC)*

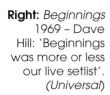

Right: *Beginnings* 1969 – Dave Hill: 'Beginnings was more or less our live setlist'. *(Universal)*

Ambrose Slade

fontana

Right: *Play It Loud* 1970 – Noddy Holder: 'We were too concerned with arrangements and stuff.' (*Universal*)

Left: *Slade Alive!* 1972 – Greg Shaw: 'This is one of the best live albums I've ever heard'. (*Universal*)

Left: *Slayed?* 1972
– Dave Hill: 'It was
a defining record
for us, not least
because of the
sleeve'. *(Universal)*

Right: *Sladest*
1973 – Plans for a
new studio album
were delayed,
although it was
an opportune
moment for a
compilation.
(Universal)

Right: *Old New Borrowed & Blue* 1974 – Ken Barnes: 'Combine melodicism with savage, wild rockers and you've got an unbeatable band'. *(Universal)*

Left: *Slade In Flame* 1974 – Dave Hill: 'When you're dealing with a soundtrack, now's the time you can afford to be a little bit ahead'. *(Universal)*

Left: *Nobody's Fools* 1976 – Don Powell: 'I like the sound on that, and it was a bit different for us'. (*Universal*)

Right: *Whatever Happened To Slade from 1977* – Jim Lea: 'The guitar player was a big thing'. (*Universal*)

Right: *Slade Alive Vol. 2* 1978 – K. Massey: 'Somewhat unknown today seems very strange, but times change and believe it or not, Slade have'. *(Universal)*

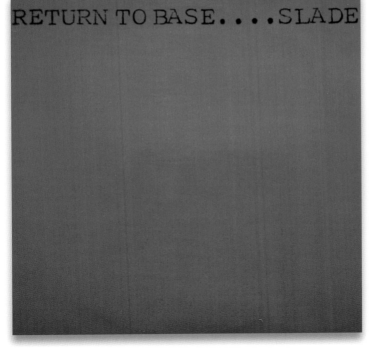

Left: *Return To Base* 1979 – Dave Hill: 'I'm very satisfied with it. It's got a mixture of different types of songs on it'. *(Barn)*

Left: At the height of the glam era, Slade featured on the front cover of scores of teen publications. (*John Barker collection*)

Right: A glitter-festooned Dave Hill on the cover of *Popster* magazine 1973. (*John Barker collection*)

Right: *Slade In Flame* tie-in novel 1975 – John Pidgeon took the screenplay and made it even darker. *(Panther)*

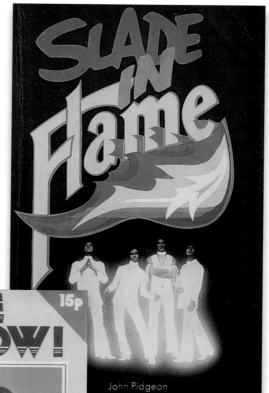

Left: *Slade Supershow* giant poster 1973. *(John Barker collection)*

This page: Slade on *Top Of The Pops in 1971* to promote 'Coz I Luv You' – their first number 1 hit. *(BBC)*

Right: Dave Hill and Jim Lea *on Top Of The Pops* with 'Merry Xmas Everybody' in December 1973, the finale to an incredible year for Slade. *(BBC)*

Above and right: Not a huge hit at the time, but now cited as one of their finest songs. Slade perform 'How Does It Feel' on *Russell Harty Plus, in* February 1975. *(ITV)*

Left and below: The collectable stickers company, Panini, produced a set of Slade stickers as part of their 1974 *Picture Pop* collection – Jim Lea ...

25 A TOP SELLERS PRODUCTION

© TOP SELLERS LTD. 1974
PRINTED IN ITALY BY PANINI-MODENA

JIMMY LEA
Date of birth: 14th June, 1952. Place of birth: Wolverhampton. Colour of eyes: Blue. Colour of hair: brown. Height: five feet ten inches. Plays: bass guitar, piano and violin.

26 A TOP SELLERS PRODUCTION

© TOP SELLERS LTD. 1974
PRINTED IN ITALY BY PANINI-MODENA

NODDY HOLDER
Real name: Neville Holder. Born: 15th June, 1950. Height: five feet eight inches. Eyes: blue. Hair: blond. Birthplace: Walsall. Lead singer with group and also plays guitar and flute.

PEEL BACK
PROTECTIVE
BACKING

... Noddy Holder ...

... Dave Hill ...

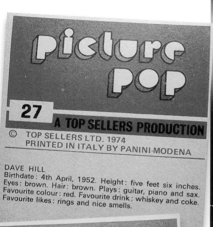

... and Don Powell.
(Darren Johnson collection)

Left: *Slade Smashes* 1980 – In the wake of the band's Reading comeback, the compilation reached number 21 in the UK charts. *(Universal)*

Right: This 2007 double-disc CD compilation finally brought together Slade's B-sides, many of which had been left off albums at the time. *(Salvo)*

Left: *Slade At The BBC* 2009 – At the start of the 1970s, Slade frequently visited BBC studios at Maida Vale. *(Salvo)*

Right: *All The World Is A Stage* 2022 – The five-disc box set includes Slade's legendary Reading performance. *(BMG)*

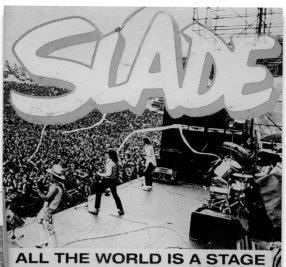

Below: By 1978, the once unbeatable Slade were playing at cabaret clubs like the Aquarius in Chesterfield. *(Simon Kimmins collection)*

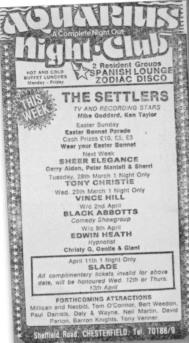

Right: *Story of Slade* 1975 – The first Slade biography written by local politician and music journalist, George Tremlett. *(Futura)*

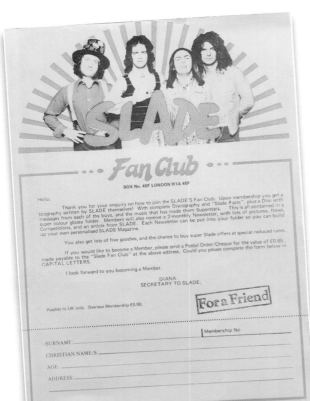

Left: A Slade Fan Club application form 1974-5. *(Darren Johnson collection)*

Below: Individual celebrations as the 2020 *Cum On Feel The Hitz* compilation goes to number eight in the UK charts. *(Collage by John Barker, Slade Are For Life - Not Just For Christmas)*

would be enforcing a three-day week from midnight on 31 December. Companies were to be permitted to consume electricity on only three consecutive days a week, additional working hours were to be banned, and TV companies were required to cease broadcasting at 10:30 pm each night. Heath declared ominously: 'In terms of comfort, we shall have a harder Christmas than we have known since the war'. This was the Christmas in which Slade's 'Merry Xmas Everybody' was first unleashed into the world.

'When Slade get hold of a Christmas song ... inevitably it's something different', said *Record Mirror*, while *Disc* concluded: 'It's a definite grower. After half a dozen hearings, you find yourself singing it'. It was a groundbreaking Christmas song in a number of ways. Unlike the treacly nostalgia of previous Christmas classics, Holder's lyric managed to capture the essence of a working-class family Christmas:

Are you waiting for the family to arrive?
Are you sure you've got the room to spare inside?
Does your granny always tell you that the old songs are the best?
Then she's up and rock-'n'-rolling with the rest

That was combined with a genuine spirit of bright, breezy optimism:

So here it is, Merry Christmas
Everybody's having fun
Look to the future now
It's only just begun

As the chorus makes clear, it is very much a song for the new year – looking ahead to the future – and not simply one about Christmas. The delivery still sounds fresh 50 years later. While it could be argued that anything Slade released at this particular time was destined to be number one, there was something marvellously subversive about the Christmas single being their best-selling record so far – people singing along to a chorus celebrating having fun, and looking to the future in the middle of a heated political standoff, a major breakdown in industrial relations and a bleak-looking new year indeed. The three-day week came into force on New Year's Day, 1974. The Christmas song that was the antidote to it, remained at number one until well January, and it was February before it dropped out of the charts.

As well as being number one in the UK and Ireland, it also reached the top five in Belgium, Germany, the Netherlands and Norway. The single has been a frequent mainstay of the UK charts in the succeeding holiday seasons, also appearing on countless Christmas compilations.

The B-side 'Don't Blame Me' has the trademark Holder yell and a pounding rhythm. All the ingredients for another slice of classic Slade raunch appeared to be there, but it remains a difficult song to love. Lacking the warmth of other Slade tracks – even the most raunchy, hard-rocking ones – it comes across as more of an angry shout-fest and is a rare misfire from the band in this period. But who cares? The band delivered an enduring classic A-side, and no one could possibly have guessed just how much it would endure.

Slade ended the year by performing 'Cum On Feel The Noize' and 'Merry Xmas Everybody' on the Christmas Day *Top Of The Pops*, sharing the studio with Suzi Quatro, The Sweet, Gary Glitter and Wizzard in what had been a truly magnificent year for glam. Despite tragedy and trauma, 1973 had been a triumphant year for Slade. Never again would they hit the same commercial peaks. But there was plenty of life left in the band, and plenty to look forward to in 1974.

Chapter Six: 1974 – Seeing The Yellow Lights

1974 would begin with an open verdict being delivered at the inquest for Powell's girlfriend Angela Morris, who was killed in the crash. Coroner Walter Forsyth was reported in the *Birmingham Post* as telling the jury: 'There is no evidence at all as to how this car was being driven. You may not feel sure, in fact, *who* was driving it'. There would be little respite for Slade that year. They would continue an exhausting schedule of touring, recording and promotion, as well as starting a brand-new venture for the band: making a film.

Much of January and early February saw them again touring the US. Commencing on 9 January in Philadelphia and concluding on 2 February at the Ambassador Theatre in St. Louis, the band shared bills with the likes of Jo Jo Gunne, Iggy Pop and The Stooges, The James Gang, Brownsville Station and Montrose. Chris Charlesworth was dispatched to the US on behalf of *Melody Maker*:

> They're on the up-and-up in the States, even though they're not in the big league yet. They're comfortably filling the smaller halls (though even these are big by British standards), they're topping the bill and getting encores, and they're beginning to get the audience participation going like they do in England. They have to work a little harder for it to happen, though, but the message is coming across. But – and it is still a big but – they haven't exactly gone-a-bomb record-wise. They've sold very few albums or singles here, despite rave reviews in the majority of US rock journals – a state of affairs that seems to mystify Manager Chas Chandler: a man who generally knows all the answers.

A short second tour of Australia followed, along with several concerts in Japan. Gillian Mayne of the *Sydney Morning Herald* reviewed the first of two Sydney shows on 21 February, noting with a touch of hyperbole: 'They played some of their best hits with vigour, including 'Gudbuy T' Jane' and 'Look Wot You Dun', bringing tears to the eyes of hundreds of tinselled schoolgirls. Their appeal to 10 and 12-year-olds is phenomenal, surpassing even Beatlemania's heyday'. Reviewing the 26 February concert in Melbourne, Bruce Guthrie of *The Herald* was unimpressed, writing sniffily: 'Festival Hall rocked as never before, with hardly a seat being occupied, as most danced in aisles or clamoured near the stage. But the group obviously lacks creativity, and no amount of sound amplification can hide their musical limitations forever'. The UK's *Daily Mirror* sent journalist Bob Hart to Tokyo's Sun Plaza for the tour's last show on 13 March: 'A full house of 4,000 Japanese youngsters were stomping out their enthusiasm for Slade. An official took me beneath the auditorium to show me what a pounding the hall's supporting girders were taking'. America might have been slow in latching onto Slade, but there was certainly no shortage of enthusiasm elsewhere.

Old New Borrowed And Blue album (1974)

Personnel:
Noddy Holder: lead vocals, rhythm guitar
Dave Hill: lead guitar, backing vocals
Jim Lea: bass, piano, guitar, backing vocals, lead vocals (2)
Don Powell: drums
Additional personnel:
Tommy Burton: piano (4)
Studio: Olympic, London, 1973
Producer: Chas Chandler
Release date: UK: February 1974
Chart places: UK: 1, US: 168
Running time: 37:32

> Within the album, there are two or three things which aren't typical Slade songs, that they've had written for a couple of years but weren't right for them at the time.
> (*Slade Fan Club* newsletter, January-February 1974)

The release of a new album was delayed by Powell's hospitalisation the previous summer. The *Sladest* compilation had plugged the gap but in early 1974, fans could finally enjoy a new studio album. *Old New Borrowed And Blue* took its title (from the old wedding-day rhyme) because of the album's mix of material, including a cover version and a handful of tracks already heard on singles. Hill was not in the studio for all of the sessions, and some of the guitar parts were played by Lea.

Released in a gatefold with side-profile head shots on the front – and similarly with their faces in full view on the back – the photography was again by Gered Mankowitz. While perhaps not as iconic as the previous *Slayed?* album, it is still a pretty iconic cover for a pretty iconic album.

'Just Want A Little Bit' (Thornton, Bass, Washington, Brown, Thompson)
The 'borrowed' part of the album title, this song was originally recorded in 1959 by Roscoe Gordon, becoming a US R&B hit in 1960. The authorship remains contested, with Gordon listed as the songwriter when it was originally released but the names listed above appearing on later versions. It was covered by America's Roy Head and Northern Ireland's Them in the mid-1960s, but Slade bring a hitherto-untapped wildness to it, making it completely their own; Holder's voice dropping to a whisper at some points, then bouncing back with unrestrained force. It is a superb album opener. Incidentally, Chandler and The Animals recorded a far-more-pedestrian version for their 1977 reunion album *Before We Were So Rudely Interrupted*.

'When The Lights Are Out' (Holder, Lea)
The first 'new' track was also the first Slade song to feature Lea on lead vocals – 'A softer version of the Holder roar', as *NME* put it at the time, also acknowledging that he made 'a nice job of it'. It was released as a single in the US, b/w 'How Can It Be'. Lea and his brother Frank re-recorded it in 1979 for the side-project The Dummies.

'My Town' (Holder, Lea)
This was the first 'old' track, given that it had been released the previous autumn as the B-side of 'My Friend Stan'. 'My Town' is a classic slice of Slade.

'Find Yourself A Rainbow' (Holder, Lea)
This was one of the real surprises for anyone expecting a whole album of amped-up, glammed-up rock-and-roll raunch. It is a slice of old-fashioned ragtime vaudeville, featuring renowned Midlands jazz pianist Tommy Burton – a well-known Black Country figure from Bilston, Wolverhampton, who passed away in September 2000.

'Miles Out To Sea' (Holder, Lea)
According to *NME*'s Keith Altham – who got a work-in-progress preview of the album in September 1973 – "Miles Out To Sea' is the saga which Nod wrote following a traumatic party for the group, held by a freaked-out citizen of San Francisco after they appeared at Winterland. The party was held in the gent's private home – a converted synagogue where a

rope suspended from the domed ceiling provided a swinging time for all'. This mid-tempo number, with a gorgeous and infectious melody, nice guitar licks and a lovely bass line, is a real album highlight. As with 'When The Lights Are Out', Lea's side project The Dummies later revisited it.

'We're Really Gonna Raise The Roof' (Holder, Lea)
Another archetypal Slade track, lyrically and sonically. Ken Barnes of *Phonograph Record* called it a 'slapdash compendium of '50s rock-and-roll clichés.' This was actually meant as a compliment from Barnes! Where would 1970s glam be without its 1950s rock and clichés?

'Do We Still Do It' (Holder, Lea)
Another typical Slade anthem with a good-time lyric, a catchy chorus and camp backing vocals, 'Do We Still Do It' is another album highlight. The *NME* deemed it one of the album's prime contenders for single status, though apparently, the band never considered it as such.

'How Can It Be' (Holder, Lea)
The tempo changes with 'How Can It Be'. The laid-back, semi-acoustic, country rock flavour was a style the band explored more-fully on their 1976 album. *Nobody's Fools*.

'Don't Blame Me' (Holder, Lea)
Another 'old' track, 'Don't Blame Me' was the 'Merry Xmas Everybody' B-side. While Slade had tended to avoid filling albums with singles and B-sides, there was a shortage of material after Powell's accident set the recording schedule back. But it is a pity that superior 1973 B-sides like 'I'm Mee, I'm Now And That's Orl' and 'Kill 'Em At The Hot Club Tonight' were passed-over in favour of this angry track that has plenty of raunch, but lacks Slade's usual warmth.

'My Friend Stan' (Holder, Lea)
Another 'old' track, this was the previous autumn's single, and the first recorded following Powell's crash.

'Everyday' (Holder, Lea)
The obvious 'blue' track, this beautiful, melancholy piano ballad was the clear standout track, and is one of Slade's best-loved slow songs. At

the *An Audience With Jim Lea* event (at Bilston, Wolverhampton's Robin 2 venue in 2017), Lea revealed that he wrote the song with his wife Louise, who came up with the words and the melody of the opening lines.

> Every day when I'm away
> I'm thinking of you
> Everyone can carry on
> Except for we two

Lea said: 'She should have a credit now, I think'. Lea wrote the bulk of the song at the piano, and Holder helped complete it. He reflected in his 1999 autobiography: 'It was the first time one of our songs had been written on a piano, so it sounded quite unusual for us'. When it came to recording, Hill was unavailable, so Lea played the exquisite guitar solo.

'Good Time Gals' (Holder, Lea)

With a lyric packed with enough double entendres to be a *Carry On* script, the album ends on a characteristically-upbeat note. Reviews at the time compared the track with The Rolling Stones' 'Honky Tonk Women'. 'Good Time Gals' was the B-side of the 'Everyday' single. Warner Bros. released it in the US as a single A-side b/w 'We're Really Gonna Raise The Roof', though it did not chart.

In the US, the Warner Bros. album had a similar cover but was retitled *Stomp Your Hands, Clap Your Feet*, and omitted 'My Friend Stan' and 'My Town', which had already appeared on the US issue of *Sladest*.

The *NME* was only partially satisfied with the album: 'One day, if they hold it together, Slade will make a cosmic album. This isn't it, but it takes care of business for now, and points encouragingly to the future'. In a review titled 'Sizzling Slade', the *Daily Express* deemed the album to be a 'good buy', arguing that Slade 'combine glimpses of Beatles harmonies with their very own brand of simple-yet-effective lyrics'.

In the US, Ken Barnes of *Phonograph Record* wrote of *Stomp Your Hands, Clap Your Feet*: 'Combine melodicism with savage, wild rockers, and you've got an unbeatable band, and Slade continue to churn out the ravers'. *Cashbox* heralded it 'another powerful collection of 'toons' ... raw power is the most immediate sensation you feel from the LP.'

While other glam singles acts like Sweet and Suzi Quatro often struggled to make an impact on the album charts, Slade were facing no such problem. This was their third consecutive UK number one, and it also reached the top ten in Australia, Norway, Finland and Sweden. But there was no sign of that prized US breakthrough yet, with the album struggling to reach just 168 in *Billboard*.

Everyday single
Personnel:
Noddy Holder: lead vocals, rhythm guitar
Dave Hill: lead guitar, backing vocals
Jim Lea: bass, guitar, piano, backing vocals
Don Powell: drums
Studio: Olympic, London, 1974
Producer: Chas Chandler
Release date: UK: March 1974
Chart places: UK: 3

'Everyday' (Holder, Lea) b/w **'Good Time Gals'** (Holder, Lea)
For Slade's next single, the stand-out ballad from Old New Borrowed And Blue was lifted from the album. At the 2017 *Audience With Jim Lea* event, Lea told fans that at the time that he was very-much against the release of 'Everyday' as a single: 'Chas and I were having a massive argument. I didn't want 'Everyday' out. I thought it was too slow. I wanted something else out'. Chandler won. It was an inspired choice. Glam rock had grown exponentially since 1971, and by 1973 had completely dominated the charts – but it would soon begin to fray. The Sweet, Mud and Suzi Quatro each began 1974 with very glam-sounding hits ('Teenage Rampage', 'Tiger Feet' and 'Devil Gate Drive' respectively). The glam sound would not be dominating the charts for much longer, however. It made sense for Slade to begin expanding their musical horizons, even if 'Everyday' wasn't quite as big a hit as most of their earlier singles.

The *Disc* review said, 'Wow! Slade singles aren't usually as individual as this one. If you're expecting the usual raucous vocals and a real rocking background, forget it. This is a lovely song, sung with considerable feeling by Noddy'. The fact that the single and its B-side had already appeared on the album only a month earlier, probably put a dent in sales, but it still notched up a number three position in the

UK, and reached the top 5 in Ireland, the Netherlands and Norway. In Australia, the A-side and B-side were reversed.

There were the inevitable *Top Of The Pops* appearances, and slots on the BBC's *Clunk Click* (the precursor to *Jim'll Fix It* hosted by the now-reviled Jimmy Savile) and Granada's *45*. In the US, the band also performed the song live on the prestigious TV music show *The Midnight Special*, along with 'My Friend Stan' and 'Do We Still Do it'.

After the single release came Slade's only 1974 UK tour, dubbed Slade's Crazee Nite tour. After spending so much time in America, the 26-date UK tour was a major undertaking, commencing at St. George's Hall, Bradford, on 19 April, culminating in three nights at London's Hammersmith Odeon from 16-18 May. In a pre-tour interview with *Disc,* Holder told Rosalind Russell that the band would not make a profit from the tour, pointing out that repair bills for the Earls Court concert alone amounted to £4,000: 'It's not wilful damage, it's just caused by kids standing on the seats. £4,000 was quite low considering there was 8,000 people there. We won't make any money out of this tour. There just aren't any halls big enough. The cost of hiring halls has gone up; we're carrying ten tons of equipment and a road crew of between 12 and 15'.

The *NME's* Roz Martini was there for the opening night in Bradford, and made the observation that it was not so much a 'Crazee Nite' as 'absolute lunacy', noting, 'The roars of both the music and the audience were deafening'. John Beattie of *Record Mirror* was there for the end of the tour, writing, 'The show was done in such a professional manner. Perhaps it's time for the boyz to change their stage image … into something more fashionable. Noddy is still the dated bovver boy, and Dave Hill dresses-up like some pouved-up version of Genesis' Peter Gabriel'.

Several decades later, such a view was echoed by Lea: 'The other thing with the band was our sort of wacky image, which we kept going on with for too long. Well, not *we*, but Dave did. You know, look at Quo back when they did 'Ice In The Sun' and they changed the way they looked to do a different thing; same as The Beatles changed, but you know that never happened with us'.

Following the UK tour, it was back across the Atlantic for another US tour. Robert V. Weinstein of *Rolling Stone* was at the New York Felt Forum gig on 31 May 1974 and was another US music journalist apparently immune to Slade's charms:

The sound equation seems to be right, but everything else is wrong. For the most part – and despite some pleasant harmonies between Holder and Dave Hill – Slade's music has not taken off in any new direction. Most of their songs are constructed on slim and unsubstantial threads of melody, and cemented together with lyrics bound by timeworn cliches.

Later on that tour, Lyne Van Matre of the *Chicago Tribune* reviewed the 21-June gig at the Chicago Auditorium, but was no-more enthusiastic: 'They are – to tell the truth – just awful. In fact, Slade comes across in many ways as Britain's retaliation to Grand Funk Railroad ... To Slade's credit, the boys' reach never exceeds their grasp. They have their formula and they stick to it, song after simplistic song'. Slade certainly needed to exhibit some considerable staying power if they were to make a success of America. Would it all be worth it?

The Bangin' Man single

Personnel:
Noddy Holder: lead vocals, rhythm guitar
Dave Hill: lead guitar, backing vocals
Jim Lea: bass, backing vocals, piano (B-side)
Don Powell: drums
Studio: Olympic, 1974
Producer: Chas Chandler
Release date: UK: June 1974
Chart places: UK: 3, US: -

'The Bangin' Man' (Holder, Lea) b/w **'She Did It To Me'** (Holder, Lea)

Rightly surmising that the *Old New Borrowed And Blue* album had been bled dry in terms of single potential, Slade returned to Olympic to record new material. 'The Bangin' Man' is not about drummer Powell as the title might suggest but is a life-on-the-road song inspired by the daily routine of Slade's tour manager Graham Swinnerton, who had to bang on each band member's hotel-room door after a heavy night of post-gig partying, to get them up and off to their next destination. After the three slightly-more-mellow previous singles, this one was back to full-throttle Slade.

However, the B-side – the beautifully poignant ballad 'She Did It To Me' – is perhaps the best non-album B-side the band ever released. It can be viewed as a companion piece and lyrical follow-up to 'Everyday', and appears to address the same lover. But the love that 'won't die' in the former song appears to have hit a brick wall:

> Cos I knew that soon we'd dry
> 'Everyday' will tell you why

Like 'Everyday', 'She Did It To Me' definitely had the qualities needed for a memorable, heartfelt hit, but Slade were wise to the fact that they could not release another ballad so soon after 'Everyday', and that it was time to hit the fans with a blast of what the band were best known for.

In their review of 'The Bangin' Man', the *NME* accused Slade of borrowing the riff from both 'Honky Tonk Women' and Free's 'All Right Now', but acknowledged that the song was 'a beaut' and part of a 'phased return to normality'. This was the first Slade single in several years that wasn't rewarded with *Top Of The Pops* appearances for the simple fact that the programme was off the air from late June to early August due to industrial action. It meant the single got less exposure than the others, but like its predecessor, it still reached number three in the UK and chalked up a handful of top ten placings elsewhere.

Following the conclusion of the US tour on 30 June, and the single release, Slade were to have a relatively low profile for several months as they set to work on making the film *Flame* and recording its soundtrack, which was released later that year as *Slade In Flame*. Holder looked back on that period in a 1999 *Q* magazine interview:

> People wanted us to do a slapstick *Hard Day's Night*-type comedy, but we really weren't keen. It seemed too obvious, so Chas commissioned a lot of script treatments. One of the first things we considered seriously was from John Steel, who came up with the idea of doing a spoof on the *Quatermass* films. I would've been Dr. Quite-a-mess, which I was very keen on, but the monster killed Dave Hill in the first 15 minutes, so that ruled it out.

In the end, the film moved in a completely different direction, becoming a gritty, hard-hitting portrayal of the music industry through the eyes of the fictional band Flame. Though a select number of fan-club members got the chance to appear in the film crowd scenes at London's Rainbow and Hammersmith Palais venues, the first public taste of Slade's new venture came on 11 October with the release of their next single.

Far Far Away single

Personnel:
Noddy Holder: lead vocals, rhythm guitar
Dave Hill: lead guitar, backing vocals
Jim Lea: bass, organ, backing vocals
Don Powell: drums
Studio: Olympic, London, 1974
Producer: Chas Chandler
Release date: UK: October 1974
Chart places: UK: 2

'Far Far Away' (Holder, Lea) b/w **'O.K. Yesterday Was Yesterday'** (Holder, Lea)

In his autobiography, Holder described the first *Slade In Flame* single 'Far Far Away' as 'probably' his favourite Slade song. He said the idea for it came to him while sitting with Chandler on a hotel balcony in Memphis, as the pair watched the Mississippi's illuminated paddle steamers sail by below: 'We had been away from home for ages, and were both feeling pretty homesick. I was talking about the things we'd seen on tour and what we'd missed back home. Then the intro of this tune just popped into my head. I started drunkenly singing it to Chas. He said, 'Go to your room now and write that down''.

In a 2020 *Vive Le Rock* interview, Lea remembered things slightly differently: "Far Far Away' I came up with when we were in a hotel on the Mississippi. I gave Nod the first line and the melody and said 'Come back with something wistful''. Holder certainly achieved that, with references to the singer's favourite spot in Paris ('I've seen the Paris lights from high upon Montmartre'), the band's early adventures in the Caribbean ('The Grand Bahama island stories carry on') and Elvis' Graceland mansion ('I've passed the 'Hound Dog'-singer's home'). From the unforgettable drum intro, to the mellow acoustic guitar, to the gorgeous solo, to Holder's seen-it-all-done-it-all but wistfully-homesick lyric, to a chorus that begs to be sung along to, every single second of the song is absolute perfection.

The B-side 'O.K. Yesterday Was Yesterday' was another song from the forthcoming film, and featured some American-sounding and very un-glam-sounding slide guitar (later explored more fully on the *Nobody's Fools* album). With its unsentimental live-for-the-moment philosophy, the track was quite a contrast to the A-side.

Awarding 'Far Far Away' their 'Pick of the Week' accolade, *Record Mirror* gave a deservedly enthusiastic review: 'This is a very melodic Noddy; no screaming or shouting; practically gentle by Slade standards, but it's very good; strong chorus line and backing. Just the name Slade normally means an instant hit. In this case, it'll be a well-deserved hit'. The band clocked up a string of *Top Of The Pops* slots, also appearing on Granada's *Lift Off With Ayshea*, and the Netherlands' *Top Pop*, where they wore the reflective white suits seen in the film *Flame* and on the album cover. The single reached number two in the UK and Ireland, and was Slade's first number one hit in Norway. They still had the ability to chalk up huge chart hits: for the time being at least.

Slade In Flame album (1974)

Personnel:
Noddy Holder: lead vocals, rhythm guitar
Dave Hill: lead guitar, backing vocals
Jim Lea: bass, piano, organ, backing vocals
Don Powell: drums
Additional personnel:
Bud Beadle: baritone saxophone
Ron Carthy, Eddie Quansah: trumpet
Mick Eve, Steve Gregory: tenor saxophone
Malcolm Griffiths, Chris Hammer Smith: trombone
Chris Mercer: baritone, tenor saxophone
Studio: Olympic, London, 1974
Producer: Chas Chandler
Release date: UK: November 1974
Chart places: UK: 6, US: 93
Running time: 41:20

> We put in a lot of hard work on this film. Jimmy and I wrote most of
> the songs for it while we were on the last tour, and concentrated hard
> on writing really good songs.
> (Noddy Holder, *Disc*, September 1974)

Recorded at Olympic in the summer of 1974, Slade had the challenge of creating songs for the fictional group Flame, whose four members the band played in the film. Given that the film was set in the late-1960s, the material could not simply be a retread of their glam sound either. It had to have a slightly different quality to what came from them before, yet, at the same time still be identifiably Slade. The album *Slade In Flame* was the result. With a brass section courtesy of British R&B band Gonzalez (who backed a host of R&B, funk and soul stars throughout the 1970s and early-1980s), and a range of influences and textures not previously heard on a Slade album, *Slade In Flame* remains a credible pointer that there would be life for the band beyond the glam era. Hill enthused to *Melody Maker's* Colin Irwin in October 1974: 'We've got some saxes and some heavy stuff in it, and a theme tune which is very obviously different for Slade. When you're dealing with a soundtrack, now's the time you can afford to be a little bit ahead'.

Again by photographer Gered Mankowitz, the album cover bore an extremely striking image of the band dressed in white, glowing against a black background. It wasn't their usual glam stage garb, but it *was* exceptionally glamorous.

'How Does It Feel' (Holder, Lea)

If 'Far Far Away' remains Holder's favourite Slade song, then it is the album's second hit single that Lea awards that personal accolade to. As he revealed at the 2017 *An Audience With Jim Lea* event: 'The best song I ever wrote was the first song I ever wrote, when I was about 13, which was 'How Does It Feel''. The song plays a prominent role in the film soundtrack. It is heard in the opening and closing credits, and Lea plays snatches of it in recording-studio scenes halfway through the film.

'Them Kinda Monkeys Can't Swing' (Holder, Lea)

With its lyric about wheeling and dealing and hustling and bustling, this song reflects the overall theme of the film and its portrayal of the seedy side of the music industry. Unlike the opening track's mellow, wistful nature, this powers along ferociously, with Holder's vocal at full throttle and Hill playing some superb slide guitar. In the film, the fictional band play this in a small club at their first gig as the newly-formed Flame.

'So Far So Good' (Holder, Lea)

Unlike the melancholy 'How Does It Feel', this mid-tempo song, with its chugging riff and fee-good vibe, strikes an optimistic tone from the perspective of a band enjoying its first taste of success. In the film, the song is presented as Flame's debut single and is heard on a pirate radio station as the band visit the offshore studio for an interview.

'Summer Song (Wishing You Were Here)' (Holder, Lea)
This is a light and breezy song with a holiday romance theme. In his
autobiography, Hill said that Chandler regarded the song as too 'namby-
pamby' for Slade, but it doesn't feel at all out of place on this album. In the
film, the song is another that the fictional band play to an adoring audience
– at the height of their success, just before their imminent collapse.

'O.K. Yesterday Was Yesterday' (Holder, Lea)
Fans had already heard the side-one closer when it was the B-side of 'Far
Far Away'. In the film, it is heard in the final concert scenes, alongside
'Summer Song (Wishing You Were Here)' and 'Far Far Away'.

'Far Far Away' (Holder, Lea)
Slade's most recent hit single opened side two of the original vinyl
album. In the film, it is performed as the final concert scene finale
before the fictional band set off to Brighton's Grand Hotel to implode
and promptly split up.

'This Girl' (Holder, Lea)
This funky and atypical Slade track has clavinet and stacks of brass. It
is the film's only song not performed by the fictional band Flame, but
rather by Holder's character's previous band The Undertakers. With that
band portrayed as a Screaming Lord Sutch And the Savages-type outfit,
Holder performs the song onstage inside a coffin. The film version
is a different recording, with a completely different lyric and a more-
melodramatic delivery to suit the scene's mock-horror aesthetic.

'Lay It Down' (Holder, Lea)
With this track's powerful-yet-laid-back vibe, Slade showed they were
being influenced by US guitar bands. The American flavour was a strong
pointer towards their subsequent album *Nobody's Fools,* while the lyric
took a tongue-in-cheek look at the mechanics of songwriting.

'Heaven Knows' (Holder, Lea)
This is another upbeat song with an optimistic feel and a catchy melody.
In the film, it is presented as the B-side of Flame's first single, 'So Far
So Good', and is heard as the band escape from the offshore pirate
radio station as it comes under gunfire in an elaborate-but-somewhat-
menacing publicity stunt.

'Standin' On The Corner' (Holder, Lea)

The final song is an out-and-out rocker that – except for the extensive use of brass and the fantastic sax solo – would not have been out of place on *Slayed?* or *Old New Borrowed And Blue*. As the title suggests, it is a song about prostitution:

> Standin' on the corner
> Handbag on her thigh
> Standin' in the shadows
> Giving all the boys the eye
> Does anybody wanna try?

In the film, the song is played in a concert scene, where Slade fan club members doubled as fanatical Flame supporters.

Tackling the Flame/Slade identity issue, *Disc* magazine's Rosemary Horride reassured fans: 'The music included here certainly sounds like the Slade we all know and love. Only occasionally do they stray from the usual mould'. Meanwhile, *Record Mirror's* Jan Iles wrote, 'Because the songs have been taken out of context, a few of them have lost their charm and meaning. But nevertheless, it's an enjoyable LP'. More challenging was Simon Frith of *Let It Rock* magazine, who saw some merit in the album but was critical of what he saw as its 'lyrical sogginess' and Slade's 'lack of musical direction' – ultimately concluding that they should find a new producer for their next album: 'Chas Chandler has exploited to the limits what Slade have got. They need someone now to demand things from them they didn't know they had'.

In the US, Warner Bros. released the album with 'The Bangin' Man' replacing 'Summer Song (Wishing You Were Here)', and 'Thanks For The Memory' replacing 'Heaven Knows'. *Rolling Stone's* John Morthland gave the *Flame* soundtrack a rather lukewarm review, deeming it 'quite safe and pat', adding, 'There's nothing here to match – either in crude energy or good spirits – Slade songs like 'Cum On Feel The Noize' and 'Gudbuy T' Jane''.

The album did not repeat the sales success of *Slayed?*, *Sladest* or *Old New Borrowed And Blue*, but still reached a creditable 6 in the UK, going as high as 2 in Norway, but just scraping to 93 in *Billboard* in the US.

The album's release coincided with a November/December European tour, taking in Iceland, Denmark, Sweden, Germany, Austria, Holland, Belgium and France.

Unlike the three preceding years, there were no Slade UK number one singles in 1974. Indeed, after a tremendous run of six UK chart-toppers, there would never again be a number one single from Slade in their home country. Still, 1974 was hardly a disaster by any stretch of the imagination. The band had clocked up two number three singles, a number two single and a number one album, with *Slade in Flame* comfortably reaching the top ten. They had still to fulfil their ambition of cracking America, but for Slade, 1975 looked bright.

Chapter Seven: 1975 - Thanks For The Memories

By 1975, musical fashions had changed considerably since Slade first began having hits four years previously. Historian Alwyn W. Turner surveyed the 1975 music scene in *Glam Rock: Dandies In The Underworld* (2013):

> At its peak, glam had kept the nation's youth supplied with beauty and danger, fantasy and fun. The charts were now full of disco and British groups recreating the high-school pop of the Kennedy years: the Bay City Rollers, Rubettes and Showaddywaddy.

Even for those glam-rock acts that still saw some chart action in 1975, the thunderous glitter beats, echoing handclaps and chanted choruses that defined the earlier hits, now gave way to newer sounds. By 1975, Sweet had dropped the 'The' from their name, ditched their songwriting team and moved into more-straight-ahead melodic hard-rock territory; Suzi Quatro released a funk album, and The Glitter Band had begun experimenting with Beach Boys-esque soft rock and pumping disco tracks. Slade, too had undergone a considerable metamorphosis. But it raised the question of whether things were moving just a little too fast for many of the fans.

How Does It Feel single
Personnel:
Noddy Holder: lead vocals, rhythm guitar
Dave Hill: lead guitar, backing vocals
Jim Lea: bass, piano, organ, backing vocals
Don Powell: drums
Additional personnel:
Bud Beadle: baritone saxophone
Ron Carthy, Eddie Quansah: trumpet
Mick Eve, Steve Gregory: tenor saxophone
Malcolm Griffiths, Chris Hammer Smith: trombone
Chris Mercer: baritone, tenor saxophone
Studio: Olympic, London, 1974
Producer: Chas Chandler
Release date: UK: February 1975
Chart places: UK: 15, US: –

'How Does It Feel' (Holder, Lea) b/w **'So Far So Good'** (Holder, Lea)

Given it was to be one of the film's standout songs, it is perhaps not surprising that 'How Does It Feel' was released as a single to coincide with *Flame* appearing at cinemas across the UK. *Disc* called the single 'one of Slade's best', predicting 'It'll go far'. *Record Mirror* also praised the single, but added a note of caution, saying it would 'be interesting to see the fans' reaction, but I don't think they'll have too much trouble succeeding'.

Backed with 'So Far So Good', it was perhaps expecting too much – releasing two songs from an album that had already sold very well since being released the previous autumn. Moreover, it raised more fundamental questions about whether this was really what record buyers were looking for in a Slade single at that time. In *Glam Rock: Music In Sound And Vision* (2018), culture academic Simon Philo cited this and Sweet's eight-and-a-half-minute version of 'The Man With The Golden Arm', to question whether these two erstwhile glam-rock acts were trying too hard to distance themselves from the teen fan bases that had been instrumental in their breakthroughs, and whether 'the changes being made were being undertaken a little too rapidly to bring those fans along for the ride'. In his 1999 autobiography, Holder made a similar point: 'It was a hit, but not a huge success ... although it's now cited as one of our finest songs. It just didn't work that well as a pop single in its own right'. In the end, the single reached 15 in the UK: Slade's lowest chart position since their 1971 breakthrough single. Nevertheless, 'How Does It Feel' still netted a trio of *Top Of The Pops* appearances, and slots on the chat show *Russell Harty Plus* and the kids' show *Crackerjack*.

The film itself premiered in Newcastle on 12 January, going on general release in the north-east and Yorkshire ahead of an official London premiere on 13 February, before being rolled-out to other regions. In a publicity stunt even dafter than some of the fictional band's stunts in the film, Slade turned up at London's Metropole Theatre on a fire engine. Interviewed by Kris DiLorenzo in an article titled 'Slade: Not As Crazee As Wee Thought' for *Good Times* magazine in the US (where *Flame* had yet to be released), Hill gave a brief synopsis:

It's a film about the hype in the business, and about a group called Flame. It shows how they're enjoying themselves, until they meet this person who wants to make 'em big stars. They're hyped-up by a big management company who wants them packaged and sold. And when he makes 'em big stars, they fall apart. They become unhappy, and they're thrown into things they don't want to do – which happens to a lot of groups: we've seen it happen.

In the same piece, Powell stressed that they wanted to do something different to what was expected of them:

We didn't want to make a chocolate-box cover, we didn't want to do the sort of everybody-jump-around-in-the-fields thing ... We wanted to portray the scene – the music industry – what it really is like for a group starting out and getting manipulated by management companies'.

In a 1999 interview with Johnny Black of *Q* magazine, Lea recalled feeling nervous about what the critics would make of it all: 'The day before the premiere, I was sitting in the Portman Hotel with my mum, when Barry Norman came on the TV and said, 'For all its failings, *Slade In Flame* has a gritty realism that you can't escape'. I breathed a huge sigh of relief'.

The film received generally-favourable reviews. *Sounds*, for example, stated: 'This film suffers less than most from the obvious imbalance of having musicians in the lead roles surrounded by experienced actors. Slade play themselves at least as well as they usually do. And in Noddy Holder in particular, they have a natural scene-stealer. *Flame* is basically the same old story, told more accurately and wittingly'.

Whether it was what the public were looking for or expecting from Slade was perhaps another matter, but with the passage of time, the film has been lauded as a classic of the genre. To accompany the film, a tie-in novel by John Pidgeon was published. With a background in scriptwriting and music journalism, Pidgeon was well-placed to transform the Slade film into a novel. While the book was based on Andrew Birkin's original screenplay, Pidgeon made it even more gritty and dark. If the film wasn't what fans expected, the novel took things a stage further, with some particularly-brutal violence and a far-more-graphic sex scene. But the book sold well, becoming the third-best-selling paperback in the *Sunday Times* list for April/May 1975.

Slade fans could content themselves with *two* books that year, as the first Slade biography was also published. In the mid-1970s,

London author George Tremlett combined being an elected member of the Greater London Council with putting out music biographies, including *The David Bowie Story*, *The Marc Bolan Story*, *The Slade Story*, and books on The Who, The Rolling Stones and various members of The Beatles. Like others in the series, the Slade book was short, undemanding and rather superficial. The pen portraits of the four members in their respective homes – which take up the middle chapters – read more like something from the lifestyle section of a glossy magazine rather than a music biography, and Tremlett repeats fictions that were common in teen magazines of the era: like several years being shaved off the band members' ages. But Tremlett maintains an enthusiasm for the band throughout, confidently predicting at the very start: 'In a few years' time, we may all be saying that Slade are the most important group to have emerged since The Beatles'.

There was another UK tour in April/May and, like whenever a Slade tour was announced, there was a plethora of press publicity, yet there was a somewhat different tone to much of the coverage this time. Beneath the headline 'Slade – Last Tour?', *Record Mirror* reported: 'Slade have announced that their forthcoming nationwide British tour will be the last in this country for at least two years. The band are to concentrate on the American market'. The other main music papers ran similar stories, while the tabloids – and even Shadow Chancellor Geoffrey Howe – focussed on the news that the band were becoming tax exiles. Holder told *The Sun's* Bob Hart: 'We don't want to go. There is nowhere else we would rather live than England, but we have no choice. If we stay, we will have to pay around 95% tax on our earnings'.

Following the wave of press coverage, Hill sought to reassure fans in a *Top Of The Pops* magazine interview that May: 'Records will continue to be released in Britain, and – if we're asked, and if our records continue to make the charts – we will either be back in person for *TOTP*, or we'll send over a film'. The following month, the *Slade Fan Club* newsletter reassured readers that 'Slade have no intention of leaving Britain permanently', citing a combination of 'crippling' UK tax rates and the need to 'conquer' America as reasons for the temporary relocation.

The tour itself attracted somewhat-mixed reviews. The *NME's* Colin Irwin saw the Bournemouth Winter Gardens gig on 18 April: 'Musically, it's not the most advanced stuff, and a hundred holes could be found in it if you looked hard enough, but that's not what a Slade concert is about'. Covering the same gig, the *Sunday Mirror* enthused that fans were 'almost raising the roof off the Winter Gardens as Slade came to the finale of their fantastic act'; concluding, 'Slade will slay 'em wherever they go'. In reviewing the 25 April gig at London's New Victoria Theatre, *Sounds*' Les Hall acknowledged that the fans 'of course adored it', but sniffily concluded that 'The lights were the only thing that held the show together'.

Fans not lucky enough or too young to have seen Slade live in this period can finally get a taste of their live set at that stage, courtesy of a recording from the New Victoria Theatre on that tour, released as part of the 2022 *All The World Is A Stage* five-CD box set. The band put in a spirited performance, with *Flame* songs ('Them Kinda Monkeys Can't Swing', 'Far Far Away', 'How Does It Feel' and 'OK Yesterday Was Yesterday') joining earlier material and the brand new single (released to coincide with the tour) 'Thanks For The Memory (Wham Bam Thank You Mam)' along with its equally-superb B-side 'Raining In My Champagne'. On the former and the piano ballad 'How Does It Feel', Lea plays an electric keyboard, though the intro to 'Everyday' is played on acoustic guitar. The recording captures an atmospheric gig, with great crowd interaction – from an important time of transition in Slade's career.

Thanks For The Memory single
Personnel:
Noddy Holder: lead vocals, rhythm guitar
Dave Hill: lead guitar, backing vocals
Jim Lea: bass, keyboards, backing vocals
Don Powell: drums
Studio: Olympic, London, 1975
Producer: Chas Chandler
Release date: UK: May 1975
Chart places: UK: 7

'Thanks For The Memory (Wham Bam Thank You Mam)'
(Holder, Lea) b/w **'Raining In My Champagne'** (Holder, Lea)
Just before Slade commenced their prolonged bout of US touring, there was one more single – the appropriately-named 'Thanks For The Memory (Wham Bam Thank You Mam)' and the final one to be recorded at Olympic. Like 'This Girl' from *Slade In Flame*, this is a funky track featuring some nifty clavinet from Lea, and an extended instrumental, while still boasting a classic sing-along chorus in the vein of 'Far Far

Away'. (The chorus melody was later reworked for 'Here's To The New Year': the B-side of Slade's 1984 Christmas hit 'All Join Hands'). Lea told *Record Mirror* at the time: 'With 'Thanks For The Memory', we really had a lot of time to spend on it, all of us worked out the arrangements and so forth. We think the overall sound is considerably more polished. We think it shows'.

The B-Side 'Raining In My Champagne' is a raucous slice of high-energy, good-time classic Slade. Though it never made it to an album, it did feature in the UK tour setlist – Jan Iles of *Record Mirror* declaring, 'This thumping, ass-blowing beat is maybe the best thing they've written in yonks'.

The *Sounds* review of 'Thanks For The Memory' deemed it 'one of their best' and 'a considerable change of pace for Slade, leaning neither to their proven hard-rock formula nor their more-recent tunefulness – while implying, at times, both of these things, whilst being – in essence – almost funky'.

Unlike the previous single, this one *did* reach the top ten: hitting number seven in the UK. But it was to be Slade's last UK-top-10 hit until 1981's 'We'll Bring The House Down' in the wake of their post-Reading comeback. The single reached an impressive 3 in Ireland, 5 in Norway, and reached the top 20 in Germany and the Netherlands. In terms of record sales, it was far from over for Slade in Europe at this point.

Throughout the latter part of 1975, they played well over 50 concerts, traversing the US for a mixture of headline dates and support slots. In July 1975 – in the early weeks of the band's prolonged US stay – Holder told *Record Mirror*'s Linda Merinof: 'We're doing everything. Sometimes we're topping the bill, sometimes we're supporting; some clubs; we'll play anywhere'. Reviewing a 21-July New York show at the Schaefer music festival, Merinoff was enthusiastic: 'Slade loves New York, and the New Yorkers at the concert wholeheartedly loved Slade. They even brought them back for a second encore after the audience lights went up, and Slade proved their gratitude for probably the biggest reception they've received in the US so far'. But reviewing the same gig for the *New York Times*, John Rockwell demonstrated that winning over US critics would be far more of a challenge:

In concert, Mr. Holder is both too smart and not smart enough. He and his band are simultaneously too tricky to sound spontaneous, and too simplistic to sound clever. Some groups can work within the limiting format of hard rock, and make you forget the limits they sell themselves on: a combination of conviction and variation within the predictable patterns. With Slade, the tension between body and brains is not so much dialectically creative, as contradictory, and the music ends up constricted and boring.

Interviewed by Bruce Meyer for the *Sarasota Herald Tribune* in August 1975, Holder acknowledged past difficulties: 'We've never been here long enough, that's the trouble. Always before, we've had commitments in Europe and England. We could come back to the US for four weeks, and then we'd have to go back. But now, we've left our book open to stay as long as we want, and we're just going to work and work and play here until everybody can see us'.

Whether it would pay off remained to be seen. In his 2013 biography, Powell drew a stark contrast between Slade's near-obsession with cracking America back then, and the attitude of another British rock band who joined them for part of that year's tour: Status Quo: 'They said, 'We are banging our heads against a brick wall in America, while losing the rest of the world. We are never coming back here again'. They had the right approach to that. If it doesn't work, why keep on trying? I honestly wish we had done the same ... While we were trying to crack America, we did neglect our big markets in Australia, England and the rest of Europe'.

Nonetheless, the UK music press still had considerable interest in Slade throughout 1975, despite them being on the other side of the Atlantic. In November-1975, *Sounds*' Geoff Barton caught up with Holder after several months' slog: 'So the live work's going great, but as far as record sales go, we haven't done a fucking thing. We haven't had AM play for our singles. We've had some FM album stuff, but nowhere near enough'. Slade attempted to rectify that with their next album – recorded in New York, and deliberately aiming for a more-American sound.

In For A Penny single
Personnel:
Noddy Holder: lead vocals, rhythm guitar
Dave Hill: lead guitar, backing vocals
Jim Lea: bass, harmonium, accordion, backing vocals, piano (B-side)
Don Powell: drums
Studio: The Record Plant, New York, 1975
Producer: Chas Chandler

Release date: UK: November 1975
Chart places: UK: 11

'In For A Penny' (Holder, Lea) b/w **'Can You Just Imagine'**
(Holder, Lea)
A foretaste of the band's US studio work came with the release of
the haunting and sublimely beautiful 'In For A Penny'. Even a bit of
characteristically tongue-in-cheek Slade smut ('tried me for size', 'bit off
more than you could chew') could not detract from the sheer elegance of
Slade's latest single. It features harmonium and accordion from Lea (with
the latter parts mimed by Holder using a concertina for TV appearances),
together with what's probably the most gorgeous guitar solo of Hill's
entire career. The B-side 'Can You Just Imagine' was an upbeat affair with
bouncy piano, big fuzzed-up guitar riffs, jazzed-up scat vocals and lyrics
inspired by the band's experience making the film *Flame*.

But the reviews were somewhat patchy. While *NME* praised Lea's
'wistful harmonium', it regarded the song as 'a bit too mellow and
tasteful'. But *Melody Maker* pulled no punches, accusing the band of
having 'a paucity of ideas', and the single of being 'weakly constructed'
and handled 'with no great enthusiasm'. Nevertheless, the band put
serious effort into promoting the single – flying back to the UK to
conduct a round of press interviews, and making TV appearances on *Top
Of The Pops* and *Supersonic*. The single went to 11 in the UK, making it
to 12 in Ireland and 14 in Sweden.

The following month saw a reissue of the band's debut 1969 album
Beginnings on the Contour label. Retitled *The Beginnings Of Slade*, and
with a new sleeve showing the band in 1970s glam garb, it could have
been an opportunity for fans to acquire the band's long-deleted early
material, but it was not to be. Chandler swiftly intervened to get the
album withdrawn. Polydor eventually reissued the original *Beginnings*
album on CD in 1991.

Although the days of straight-in-at-number-one singles were well behind
them, the garish stage-wear had been toned down and glam rock had
been and gone, 1975 was far from being a failure for Slade. New musical
influences were being explored. They could look back on a run of hit
singles, an enthusiastically-received UK tour, and a well-received film that
confounded expectations. But for the foreseeable future, Slade's fortunes
would be tied up with their determination to succeed in America. Would
Slade crack America in 1976? Or would America crack Slade?

Chapter Eight: 1976 – Calling It Quits

Slade would spend a good chunk of 1976 in pursuit of their obsession with trying to crack America. They would not neglect the UK market entirely, and would enjoy some success there with a new single and album, although they would face a spectacular flop in their second bid for the UK singles chart that year. But with no sign of an imminent breakthrough in the States, they would bid farewell to their relentless touring schedule there, and head back to Britain in late-summer 1976 to a music scene that was changing rapidly.

Let's Call It Quits single
Personnel:
Noddy Holder: lead vocals, rhythm guitar
Dave Hill: lead guitar, backing vocals
Jim Lea: bass, backing vocals
Don Powell: drums
Studio: The Record Plant, New York, 1975
Producer: Chas Chandler
Release date: UK: January 1976
Chart places: UK: 11

'Let's Call It Quits' (Holder, Lea) b/w **'When The Chips Are Down'** (Holder, Lea)
This was the second single from the forthcoming US-produced *Nobody's Fools* album. With nifty, bluesy guitar work and another elongated vibrato-laden solo from Hill, it was much more in the classic Slade mould than the mellower 'In For A Penny', though 'Let's Call It Quits' remains one of Slade's slower numbers, despite packing a punch. It bears more than a passing similarity to the Allen Toussaint song 'Play Something Sweet (Brickyard Blues)' (recorded by Three Dog Night in 1974), and Slade members have given conflicting accounts over the years about whether it resulted in any legal action or out-of-court financial settlement. The song is a tale of romantic tensions between two lovers rather than any commentary on the band leaving Britain or packing it all in.

The B-side 'When The Chips Are Down' is a fast and furious slice of classic, raucous Slade that would not have sounded out of place on the 1972 *Slayed?* album. It would certainly have stuck out had it been included on *Nobody's Fools,* but – like the previous B-side 'Can You Just Imagine' – it was left off the album.

Record Mirror gave a strong review: 'One of Slade's best – a slow, heavy rocker with rude words that are just about oblique enough to get by on any radio play'. The band again took some time out from the US to promote the single in the UK. There was an innovative promo video showing the band surrounded by mirrors, and there were TV appearances on *Top Of The Pops, Supersonic* and *Jim'll Fix It.* Like its predecessor, the single reached 11 in the UK, though it had little impact anywhere else and was not released in the US, in spite of being recorded there.

Nobody's Fools album (1976)

Personnel:
Noddy Holder: lead vocals, rhythm guitar
Dave Hill: lead guitar, backing vocals
Jim Lea: bass, piano, keyboards, backing vocals
Don Powell: drums
Additional personnel:
Tasha Thomas: backing vocals
Paul Prestotino: dobro
Studio: The Record Plant, New York, 1975
Producer: Chas Chandler
Release date: UK: March 1976
Chart places: UK: 14, US: -
Running time: 42:03

> That particular album is actually my favourite Slade album. I like the sound on that, and it was a bit different for us.
> (Don Powell, *Look Wot I Dun: My Life In Slade*, 2013)

For the recording of Nobody's Fools, Slade returned to The Record Plant in New York, where they recorded 'Merry Xmas Everybody' in 1973. Hill noted in his autobiography: 'We hadn't got a record that sounded right on American radio, so we decided that making our next album there might be a way to solve that problem'. The previous autumn, Holder told *Sounds*: 'It's a rock album, but it's not the old Slade Rock. It's completely influenced by being in America. We've spent a lot of time, a lot of care over it. There are lots of new ideas. There are some connections with the past, admittedly, but there's also a lot of new stuff'.

US singer-songwriter Tasha Thomas provide soulful backing vocals along with two other uncredited female backing singers, and session man Paul Prestotino played dobro. It is an uncharacteristically laid-back, musically interesting and highly listenable album from a time of significant change for the band.

The album title comes from one of the tracks which was later released as a single. By adding an 's' to 'fool', they repurposed what was ostensibly the title of a love song, into a commentary on the band themselves. With Gered Mankowitz' cover photography, the band celebrated their 10th anniversary by paying homage to the positions the four had adopted on their 1970 album *Play It Loud* – this time on a plain white background, and photographed from the waist up. Visually, the band have entered their post-glam phase, but are still flamboyantly dressed – with Hill in denim and studded leather, Holder in a US traffic cop's leather cap (which was soon to be made famous by Village People), Powell with a red neckerchief, and Lea with bright red braces. Playing on the album title, all four wear red noses while adopting deliberately glum expressions.

'Nobody's Fool' (Holder, Lea)
A 1981 *Slade Supporters' Club* newsletter revealed that this track was initially intended to be a '20-minute extravaganza with everything thrown in' – Lea being very much influenced by Queen at the time. That plan never came to fruition, but it is still a striking opener for a Slade album, signalling to the listener that this was *not* going to be another *Slayed?*, *Old New Borrowed And Blue* or *Slade In Flame*, but a much more mellow affair altogether. With its laid-back AOR rock vibe and soulful female backing vocals, this was Slade entering new musical territory.

'Do The Dirty' (Holder, Lea)
This begins with a loud yell. Holder explained in the *Slade Fan Club* newsletter: 'We might be doing something a bit slow, and you get all these kids screaming 'BOOGIE!'. That's why we decided to put a great big loud 'Boogie' at the beginning of 'Do The Dirty". Boogie is certainly what the track is, as the band power into some tight guitar riffing with fine funky bass playing.

'Let's Call It Quits' (Holder, Lea)
The most-recent single, released in January.

'Pack Up Your Troubles' (Holder, Lea)
Slade had dipped a toe in country rock before with 'How Can It Be' on the *Old New Borrowed And Blue*. But here the four lads from Wolverhampton achieve a pleasingly-convincing country vibe, replete with around-the-campfire acoustic guitar, dobro (courtesy of Paul Prestotino) and lyrics that include lines like catching a 'fish on the line', packing up 'your liquor and your cigarettes and your pills' and a 'freedom train comin''. The rousing Holder vocal stops it becoming overly sentimental, and – perhaps surprisingly – it all comes together rather magnificently.

'In For A Penny' (Holder, Lea)
The November 1975 single.

'Get On Up' (Holder, Lea)
One of the album's heavier tracks, the listener could be forgiven for thinking it was a return to Slade of old at their bombastic best. Only when the soulful female backing vocals kick in are we alerted to a new layer of subtlety within the classic Slade sound. It is a track to keep the more-traditional Slade fans happy, but it still fits extremely well with the album. Included in the band's live set, the song became the opener on their second live album *Slade Alive, Vol. 2,* two years later.

'L.A. Jinx' (Holder, Lea)
The band had encountered numerous problems whenever they performed live in Los Angeles, thus providing inspiration for this song. Lea told *Record Mirror*:

> Every time we go there, something goes wrong – the gear breaks down or doesn't arrive or something'.

Jinxed or not, the band came up with a sun-kissed, laid-back American sound typical of many US bands of the era, save for Holder's unmistakable vocal.

'Did Ya Mama Ever Tell Ya' (Holder, Lea)
Like a 1970s sitcom or a *Carry On* film, double entendres were never far from a Slade lyric if Noddy Holder had his way, and this song is no exception. Familiar nursery rhymes are recycled with a naughty twist, set to a reggae groove with soulful backing vocals.

Musically, it all hangs together extremely well, but it is hard to believe that the band would think lyrics like this were the key to getting airplay on the more-sophisticated AOR radio stations:

Jack and Jill went up the hill
Supposed to get some water
They stayed up there a long time
Doing what they shouldn't ought-a

What on earth were they thinking?

'Scratch My Back' (Holder, Lea)
With its big heavy riffs, powerful Holder yell and blinding Hill guitar solo, this – like 'Get On Up' – is another song in the archetypal Slade mould. Were it not for Tasha Thomas' backing vocals, it could have come from any of the three prior studio albums.

'I'm A Talker' (Holder, Lea)
As with 'Pack Up Your Troubles', this is another slice of folky Americana. Like many Slade songs before it, the lyric celebrates the art of having a good time. But rather than 'crazee mamas' and 'feeling the noize', it's about throwing logs on the fire, passing around a joint and enjoying a little bit of music. It's the Slade manifesto given a laid-back California makeover.

'All The World Is A Stage' (Holder, Lea)
This is one of the album's most experimental songs. The lyric invokes Shakespeare's famous monologue from *As You Like It*, to celebrate the art of performance and communion with one's audience. It all comes across as rather pretentious, a little overblown and curiously out of step with the album. Holder turning from Shakespeare to showbiz schmaltz at the end – 'You've been very wonderful tonight. Thank you. Good night' – does nothing to rescue it.

By the mid-1970s, no glam band was going to escape the sharp tongue of the *NME*. They might have been early champions of Slade, but by 1976 they pulled no punches. Reviewing the album for the *NME*, Tony Stewart wrote: 'Though superficial, the music is of a reasonable standard; there's not a lot of depth. Really the album is just a collection of kooky little singles ... Most of the lyrics are banal and drab'. Other reviews were more positive. Sue Byrom in *Record Mirror* praised the arrangements, which included 'some solid bass work that would've done justice to Led Zeppelin', and welcomed tracks 'that are a lot deeper than I expected'. Declaring it a 'cracking album', *Music Week* concluded that Slade were 'now playing better than ever' and have 'matured to the point of being able to convert an older audience to their cause'.

In the US, *Billboard* asserted that the band offered 'their usual lively rock with a bit more maturity than past efforts ... Songs are better, production is better, and singing and production generally seems less haphazard in approach'. *Cashbox* asserted that 'Slade's reckless-abandon approach has taken a decidedly laid-back approach', and highlighted the 'pop subtleties' and 'genuine mellow moments'.

While *Nobody's Fools* did not repeat the success of earlier hit albums, it reached an impressive number 14 in the UK – showing that Slade's album sales were holding-up quite well in the post-glam age: certainly compared to Sweet, T. Rex, Suzi Quatro and Gary Glitter. But a rude awakening came the following month when the title track was released as a single. The album reached 14 in Sweden, but despite the strong American focus, it failed to make the *Billboard* chart. It was the last time a Slade album entered the UK charts until the *Slade Smashes* compilation was released in 1980.

Nobody's Fool single
Personnel:
Noddy Holder: lead vocals, rhythm guitar
Dave Hill: lead guitar, backing vocals
Jim Lea: bass, piano, backing vocals
Don Powell: drums
Additional personnel:
Tasha Thomas: backing vocals
Studio: The Record Plant, New York, 1975
Producer: Chas Chandler
Release date: UK: April 1976
Chart places: UK: -, US: -

'Nobody's Fool '(Holder, Lea) b/w **'L.A. Jinx'** (Holder, Lea)
Following the album's release, Slade's next single was an edited version of the AOR 'Nobody's Fool'. *Record Mirror* was extremely optimistic:

'This is one of the best singles Slade have released for ages. Very catchy, from the first hearing. Bright and bouncy, and Slade at their best. Instant hit'. It was not to be. Though both of the previous singles reached a highly-respectable 11 in the UK, 'Nobody's Fool' failing to reach even the top 50 – by far the worst showing for a Slade single since 1970. For the first time since the pre-hit days, there were no TV appearances either, in spite of the band producing an impressive promo video that juxtaposed footage of the band performing the single with blue-screen effects bringing to life a succession of images referenced in the lyrics. Backed with the album track 'L.A. Jinx', the single's failure was the first sign that Slade's might be heading for serious trouble. In the US, despite huge efforts, the single – with 'When The Chips Are Down' as the B-side – did not chart at all.

After some time away from the States in early 1976 to undertake promo work and rehearsal in the UK, the band returned to the US in early-April. They recommenced touring, crisscrossing the various states – including California, Washington, Wisconsin, Missouri, Iowa, Minnesota, Milwaukee, New Jersey, New York, Ohio, Philadelphia, Illinois, North Dakota, Tennessee and Mississippi – not to mention some gigs in Ontario, British Columbia, Alberta and Manitoba, Canada. Richard Cromelin – who had reviewed the band in 1973 on their first US tour – was back to witness Slade at L.A.'s Starwood Club on 15 April for the *L.A. Times*:

Slade's promise lay in three or four songs – inspired, vibrant pop rock powered by great song progressions and an engaging dumbness. On opening night, the group played one of them during the set – one as an encore, and ignored its best 'Cum On Feel The Noize'. The bulk of the show consisted of entirely trite rockers, most of them based on standard blues patterns, jacked-up to maximum distortion level and capped with Holder's chainsaw-massacre of a voice. Slade's futility and persistence were momentarily amusing, but the group quickly achieved its inimitable blend of obnoxious manner and insipid music (and vice versa), destroying any lingering tolerance.

While the band got an excellent response at certain gigs, the reaction was decidedly cooler at others. US record sales were negligible, and the band seemed as far away from their long-awaited US breakthrough than ever. Old chart rivals Sweet were enjoying considerable success in the US at this point, with two top-30 albums and a clutch of hit singles – but it did not seem to be working for Slade. In his autobiography, Hill alluded to growing frustrations in the band: 'I don't think we understood the market we were trying to tap into, and Chas wasn't always around to help out either. He also had other things he was interested in, and we couldn't turn to him for advice or support in the way we'd been able to back home'.

Homesickness was setting in, touring the US was proving to be incredibly expensive, and with no breakthrough in sight, the band told Chandler they wanted to return to the UK. Slade flew back to Britain in August 1976. There was no big announcement heralding their return, and they quietly set about putting together a new album. There was a slightly cryptic single paragraph tucked away towards the back of the end-of-year fan-club newsletter: 'Tremendous news! The boys are back in town and in the studio recording a new album and single to be released before Christmas. They are hoping to lay down 16 tracks and pick the best to release'. In the event, fans and the public had to wait until 1977 to hear what Slade had been working on.

Chapter Nine: 1977 – Whatever Happened To Them?

Slade returned to the UK the previous summer 1976 with little fanfare, but the music scene had changed greatly while they were away. Disco and punk were now in the ascendancy. While it can be argued that the rise of punk brought a sense of urgency and excitement back to rock and roll (as glam had done in 1971), the nihilistic pose of leading punks meant that the movement had little time for acknowledging its cultural lineage, even though, as Alwyn W. Turner pointed out in *Glam Rock* (2013):

> Punk, of course, was largely populated by those who had grown up on glam, whether as musicians… or as fans.

Although Slade were under no illusions about seeing a repeat of the hysteria that followed them at the height of their glam years, they would have their work cut out for them, trying to make any kind of impact.

Gypsy Roadhog single
Personnel:
Noddy Holder: lead vocals, rhythm guitar
Dave Hill: lead guitar, backing vocals
Jim Lea: bass, backing vocals
Don Powell: drums
Studio: Advision, London, 1976
Producer: Chas Chandler
Release date: UK: January 1977
Chart places: UK: 48

'Gypsy Roadhog' (Holder, Lea) b/w **'Forest Full Of Needles'** (Holder, Lea)
This was the first release from the 1976 sessions following the band's return to the UK. Rather than heading back to Olympic Studios in Barnes, the band recorded at Advision Studios in central London. Originally founded for making advertising voice-overs and jingles, by the mid-1960s, Advision had become a favoured location for rock bands. A move from New Bond Steet to Gosfield Street in 1969 saw the studio kitted out with state-of-the-art equipment, and Slade were one of many

acts who recorded there, including David Bowie, Buzzcocks and Kate Bush. Slade also changed their record label. Still distributed by Polydor (for the time being at least), the new label was Chandler's own Barn Records, which he established in 1976.

'Gypsy Roadhog' was a catchy number with a beautiful, distinctive slide-guitar riff from Hill, and a melody that was certainly more memorable than the previous single. The song's breezy, upbeat nature stood in stark contrast to the lyric about a cocaine dealer: 'powdered my nose', 'happy dust', 'my little silver spoon'. Was this really the thing to get Slade back into the public eye and on the radio again in Britain?

The B-side was 'Forest Full Of Needles' – written 'after driving through the Canadian Rockies, where a forest fire had raged through thousands of acres of mountains', wrote Holder in his 2014 book *The World According To Noddy*.

NME remained distinctly unimpressed: 'This makes all the right sounds and even has a toe-tapping beat, but isn't a patch on the rude, offensive and entirely wonderful noise these boys made some four or five years ago. Its careful use of American place-names and general blandness could give them that desperately needed American hit. But as far as these isles are concerned, it's just the latest step in their continuing irrelevance'.

But it wasn't merely indifferent reviews that stopped the single from becoming successful. Promotion was initially positive, with one-off appearances on the children's show *Blue Peter* (with a hastily cleaned-up lyric), *Top Of The Pops* and *Supersonic*. But as controversy over the song grew, it received little airplay. It spent a week at 48 in the UK, dropping to 50 before disappearing altogether.

In 'Gypsy Roadhog' Slade had a great song with a catchy melody. It was the album's best song by a mile, but the lyric was crassly misjudged for a band looking to regain momentum after the complete failure of the previous single. Slade fans had aged, but many of them remained young teenagers. A song about a drug dealer was never going to get the airplay necessary to catapult the band back into the public eye in a Britain that still had only three TV channels and a fairly-conservative approach governing what was deemed suitable for broadcast.

Whatever Happened To Slade album (1977)
Personnel:
Noddy Holder: lead vocals, rhythm guitar
Dave Hill: lead guitar, backing vocals

Jim Lea: bass, backing vocals
Don Powell: drums, percussion
Studio: Advision, London, 1976
Producer: Chas Chandler
Release date: UK: March 1977
Chart places: UK: -
Running time: 40:40

The *Whatever Happened To Slade* album came out of us touring in
America. There were a lot of bands out there that had this guitar
identity. There was the Allman Brothers with Duane Allman; there
was ZZ Top coming through. The guitar player was a big thing, so we
started coming up with *Whatever Happened To Slade*.
(***An Audience With Jim Lea*** at the Robin 2, November 2017)

This album is certainly harder and heavier than its predecessor. Indeed, it is
probably heavier than any Slade album before it, and for that reason, it has
found favour with many dedicated fans over the years. It has also been cited
as having an impact on 1990s grunge and alternative rock. However, one
alternative view – and one shared by this author – is that the album put its
sound and style ahead of the catchy melodies and memorable songwriting
that had always been the hallmark of a great Slade album. Unlike earlier
albums, there is very little, apart from 'Gypsy Roadhog', that a casual fan
could hum along to in the shower. When the album was recorded, tensions
were growing between the band and Chandler. Interviewed for Chris
Charlesworth's 1984 Slade biography *Feel The Noize* (written at the height
of their early-1980s comeback), Chandler remained critical of the band's
musical approach following their 1976 return to the UK:

It was as if they were determined to silence their critics by writing
blinding songs that would blow the knockers' minds. However, the trick
is to write songs that will blow the public's minds. Critics don't buy
records... they felt that a great sound was the all-important thing. I've
always felt that the song comes first, and you craft your sound to suit
the song, not the other way 'round'.

Chandler was certainly right in one respect – there was not one song
from this era that ever remained in Slade's live set when they began
enjoying a comeback at the start of the 1980s. Chandler may not have

been keen on the songs, but as Hill explains in his autobiography, the album title was Chandler's idea: '*Whatever Happened To Slade* was meant to be tongue-in-cheek now that we were back in the UK, but a lot of critics took it at face value'. The cover showed the band standing in front of retro posters of themselves in their skinhead period, affixed to a large wall on Rock Street, Islington.

'Be' (Holder, Lea)
While, musically, 'Be' is a relatively laid-back hard-rock track with a funky rhythm, the vocal is like rap on speed. Holder delivers the choruses at a machine-gun pace. It showed musical complexity and a willingness to experiment, and the song made it to the live setlist that year, and appeared on the *Slade Alive Vol. 2* album. But it was hardly the kind of song people were going to sing along to.

'Lightning Never Strikes Twice' (Holder, Lea)
Like the album's single 'Gypsy Roadhog', this is another drug song, but unlike that song it is anything but jaunty. Seemingly describing a nightmare hallucination from a bad trip, it doesn't sound a million miles from a heavy version of the kind of thing on *Play It Loud*. It was certainly a long way away from the sort of Slade song that celebrated the art of having a good time.

'Gypsy Roadhog' (Holder, Lea)
The album's most memorable song by a mile, it is just a shame the lyric made it such a catastrophically ill-judged choice for a single.

'Dogs Of Vengeance' (Holder, Lea)
With dark and foreboding riffs and equally dark lyrics, this is another seriously-heavy track. This slice of proto-grunge shows why the leading lights in that movement loved this album. 'Mama Weer All Crazee Now' this is not.

'When Fantasy Calls' (Holder, Lea)
This lyric returns to a more-familiar Slade theme. There has never been a shortage of innuendo in Slade lyrics, and this is no exception. Although, being from *Whatever Happened To Slade*, it is backed by more dark and broody, monster riffing. Lea's heavy bass playing is exceptional, as is Hill's lead-guitar work.

'One Eyed Jacks With Moustaches' (Holder, Lea)

This is a chugging boogie track, containing obvious influences from ZZ Top and US guitar-based bands that Lea referred to when discussing the album at the 2017 *An Audience With Jim Lea* event. But it retains enough of the classic Slade sound to make it unmistakably them. One of the album's more-entertaining tracks, it contains a wonderful Elvis-esque rockabilly vocal interlude from Holder.

'Big Apple Blues' (Holder, Lea)

This is a warts-and-all celebration of life in New York was – like the rest of the album – written when the band were still based in the US. In 1979, Slade's old glam rivals Sweet paid similar homage with their track 'Big Apple Waltz'. But where was a genteel piano ballad, Slade's offering is a hard, driving slice of guitar rock.

'Dead Men Tell No Tales' (Holder, Lea)

More melodic, and somewhat lighter in tone than the rest of the album, this is the story of a bank robbery gone wrong – said to be based upon the 1949 gangster movie *White Heat*, which starred James Cagney.

'She's Got The Lot' (Holder, Lea)

This one is a celebration – from the point of view of a male admirer – of a woman who has everything. It carries echoes of the equally-slow-and-brooding and similarly lyrically lascivious 'Get Down And Get With It' B-side 'Do You Want Me', though this is much heavier.

'It Ain't Love But It Ain't Bad' (Holder, Lea)

This track is built around Powell's powerful drumming, which heralds the start of the song. With some mean and dirty riffing, the lyric is about a particular aspect of life on the road for the 1970s male rock star: groupies.

'The Soul, The Roll And The Motion' (Holder, Lea)

The album concludes powerfully with more hard, pounding riffs and ferocious vocals from Holder, with little regard for notions of the commercial or being radio-friendly. Virtually any of these tracks would have made for fine, hard, uncompromising riff-based rock on any Slade album. But whether we needed a whole album of them, was another matter entirely.

Sounds' Pete Makowski grasped exactly what the album was aiming to do, and gave an enthusiastic review: 'The album is high energy on a primeval scale. It's got all the ball-bustin' riffs you'll find nestling comfortably alongside yer ZZ Tops and Nugents'. *Record Mirror'*s Shelia Prophet was less sympathetic: 'Part of the problem seems to be that they are trying too hard – laying everything on, instead of sticking with simplicity. The result is that it all sounds heavy, cluttered, even (dare I say it) a bit old-fashioned. Noddy's voice still sounds great, and Dave turns in some pretty nifty guitar, but there's too much of everything'. Over at *NME*, Charles Shaar Murray was far-more scathing: 'It's loud, shrill and trebly, and sounds like Status Quo speeded-up and stuck inside a large cardboard box ... Slade were magnificent back in '72, but since then, they've wasted their energy on unsuccessful attempts to crack the States. They've been away too long, and they don't seem to be able to speak to the kid on the street in '77 the way they talked to his/ her '72 incarnation'.

The album did not chart anywhere, neither in Britain nor in mainland Europe. Unlike the previous album, which was very much aimed at an ill-fated attempt to break into the US market, this album was not even released in America.

Burning In The Heat single
Personnel:
Noddy Holder: lead vocals, rhythm guitar
Dave Hill: lead guitar, backing vocals
Jim Lea: bass, backing vocals
Don Powell: drums
Studio: Advision, London, 1976
Producer: Chas Chandler
Release date: UK: April 1977
Chart places: UK: –

'Burning In The Heat' (Holder, Lea) b/w 'Ready Steady Kids' (Holder, Lea)
Recognising that *Whatever Happened To Slade* contained little in the way of single material, and following the relative lack of success for 'Gypsy Roadhog', the band swiftly followed up the release with this non-album single. With its big riffs, catchy melody, chorus chants and risqué lyric, 'Burning In The Heat' was certainly more commercial and

bore more of the hallmarks of the old-style Slade. But it wasn't enough – the single did not chart anywhere, although it did give the band a couple of TV appearances in Germany. The single also won favour with *Sounds* reviewer Chas De Whalley: 'The dirtiest, ballsiest single of the lot. Slightly old-fashioned but disease-ridden all the same. I like it'. The song appeared in the live setlist of that year's UK tour, and can be heard on the *Slade Alive Vol. 2* album. Lea also resurrected it for his Dummies side-project, and British band Girlschool covered it on their 1983 album *Play Dirty*, which was produced by Holder and Lea.

The B-side 'Ready Steady Kids' was a hard rock number more in the vein of the recent album. Written about the band's experiences touring the US, if 'Cum On Feel The Noize' was all about their over-exuberant early-1970s British audiences, then 'Ready Steady Kids' was more about the laid-back and typically-stoned American audiences the band were playing to by the mid-1970s:

> The ready steady kids are flippin' their lids and rippin' their skids – look out!
> The ready steady kids are pickin' their sticks and smokin' their cigs

In mid-April, Slade left for a short tour of Norway and Denmark. Getting a favourable press reaction in Scandinavia was clearly seen as important ahead of an 11-date UK tour planned for the following month. The *NME* noted that Polydor had invested more than £2,000 flying seven UK journalists to Copenhagen for the concert on 20 April and a series of interviews. But such lavish hospitality gave no guarantee of an easy ride when it came to reviewing that concert at Copenhagen's Falkoner Teatret. Sheila Prophet of *Record Mirror* (previously an ever-reliable champion of Slade), pulled no punches:

> Since 1975, music has moved on, changed, developed. Slade haven't. It's as simple as that. Reliving memories is fun, for a while. But sooner or later, a band – no matter how big they once were – have to prove they can move with the times and produce something new. For Slade, that time is now. At the dinner after the show, the band seem happy enough with the concert. But as the night progresses, the talk drifts back to Wolverhampton, to the early days, to past glories. Those were the days. But those *weren't* the days – *these* are the days, right now. Surely memories aren't all that Slade have left?

Melody Maker's Colin Irwin made similar noises:

> The new album is disappointing. Albums never were their strong point compared to the excitement they produce live, but tonight the sound is terrible, the music relentless; lacking the vitality they've had in the past. Their outstanding history, decrees that we give them a decent chance, but there's no way of getting around it – the question that arises is whether it may have been better to have gracefully quit while out of the limelight.

Tony Stewart of the *NME* was also less than enthusiastic:

> They play a mixture of their hits and album tracks, but the sound is appalling, and it's rare to hear either Jim Lea's bass lines or Don Powell's drumming over Dave Hill's exuberant guitar-chopping. Essentially, the fun of their special clumping brand of unpretentious rock, is missing. Noddy Holder sings well, but his usual onstage ribaldry is seldom evident, and no amount of gooning by Hill, the familiar glitter clown, can disguise a basic lack of enthusiasm.

Interviewed by Stewart after the gig, a bullish Lea was confident about regaining lost ground: 'The main thing is we're playing. Things happen, and there's nothing you can do about it. Like Ozzy Osbourne was saying last night, it's all one big circle. People come back all the time'.

Following the metaphorical mauling at the hands of the UK music press on the Scandinavian tour, the band picked up much better press on the UK tour - which began at Bristol's Colston Hall on 1 May and concluded at London's Rainbow on 12 May. (A planned Ipswich date had to be rescheduled for later in the month due to Holder suffering throat problems.) *Melody Maker's* Paul Morley positively glowed at Slade's triumph at Manchester's Free Trade Hall on 7 May: 'Everyone had a solo spot three times over, the sound was perfect, light show spot on, the crowd felt wanted, and responded with glee. It was the kind of rock-as-showbiz outing that I'd pay money to see for years to come. You can't beat professionalism and precision when it's executed with such fervour'.

Reviewing the Newcastle City Hall gig the following night, *Sounds'* Phil Sutcliffe asserted, 'Their rhythms are still colossal, and they have all come a distance as players ... I expect Slade will be the Status Quo of 1987'.

Slade got a fair bit of publicity ahead of the tour – not just in the music press but in the tabloids – though much of this centred as much on Hill's newly-shaven head as it did on the music. The guitarist's weird trademark high-cut fringe of the glam years had long gone, of course. It was replaced by a long, fuller-bodied pageboy-style in the mid-1970s, but that too was now gone and Hill was completely bald. He told biographer Chris Charlesworth in *Slade: Feel The Noize* (1984): 'It was done because of punk ... I guess I wanted to be part of it'. But Hill was far more philosophical in his 2017 autobiography: 'In the hits years, Chas said that I was always next year, this year – meaning I got there first with the image and the clothes. But now I was copying things, trying to catch up with the scene. We all were'.

Following the UK tour came a tour of Germany in the second half of May, alongside glam-era rock and roll revivalists The Rubettes. Later in the year, German fans were also able to purchase the lavish double-disc compilation album *The Story Of Slade*, which was comprised of 24 tracks spanning the years 1971-1976. UK fans would have to wait another three years for a new Slade greatest hits compilation, however.

'Burning In The Heat' was not the vehicle to get Slade back in the charts or on *Top Of The Pops*, but an unexpected tragedy that rocked the world of popular music that summer, perhaps could provide such an opportunity?

My Baby Left Me/That's Alright single

Personnel:
Noddy Holder: lead vocals, rhythm guitar
Dave Hill: lead guitar, backing vocals ('O.H.M.S.')
Jim Lea: lead guitar ('My Baby Left Me/That's Alright'), bass, backing vocals
Don Powell: drums
Studio: Advision, London, 1977
Producer: Chas Chandler
Release date: UK: October 1977
Chart places: UK: 32

'My Baby Left Me/That's Alright' (Arthur Crudup) b/w **'O.H.M.S.'** (Holder, Lea)
The death of Elvis Presley in August 1977 prompted all kinds of musical tributes, including the truly cringeworthy 'I Remember Elvis Presley

(The King Is Dead)' by Danny Mirror, which got to number four in the
UK charts that autumn. Far more tasteful (though not as successful) was
Slade's own tribute – a medley of two songs by bluesman Arthur Crudup,
which were both recorded by Presley in his early years. Slade powered
through the songs with great energy. Actually, it was three-quarters of
Slade, as Hill was unavailable for the session, and Lea played both lead
guitar and bass. The trio suitably *Sladified* these two old rock-and-roll
classics, and it made for a worthy tribute to a true rock-and-roll hero.

The B-side 'O.H.M.S.' is a furious riposte to the UK's then-current
83% top tax rate. Even the most dedicated supporter of redistributive
taxation could probably feel a degree of sympathy for bands like Slade,
who raked in serious amounts of money for a short period at the
height of their success, but were left with huge tax bills once the record
sales dried up. One can certainly understand the band's anger, but the
problem is that the track comes across as so angry that it lacks the usual
Slade charm and warmth. The Beatles' 'Taxman' makes similar points
with far-more good humour, although, of course, they probably had far
more money in their bank accounts and far less to be angry about.

While *Melody Maker* and *Record Mirror* were distinctly unimpressed
with the single, *Sounds* gave it a far more enthusiastic review: 'Fabulous
treatment of this old Arthur Crudup number could easily see Slade back
in the charts'. Though the single nowhere-near repeated the success of
Slade's glam years, *Sounds* were nearer the mark than their rivals, and
the single reached 32 in the UK charts and got the band back on *Top Of
The Pops*. Their best-ranking single in over 18 months, it would be 1981
before the band got anywhere near either the top 30 or the *Top Of The
Pops* studio again.

When glam rock first took flight in 1971, Marc Bolan and then Slade
were at the forefront. As 1977 drew to a close, Bolan was dead: tragically
killed in a car crash in September. Slade would be left wondering what
1978 had in store for them, and whether they could regain any of the
momentum that had propelled them to the top of the charts and sold-out
concerts in some of the world's largest venues only a few years earlier.

Chapter Ten: 1978 - Needing A Goal

1978 would see a revival in fortunes for two of Slade's old glam chart rivals. Sweet hit the top ten with 'Love Is Like Oxygen' in February, while two months later, Suzi Quatro got to number four with 'If You Can't Give Me Love'. Sadly, there would be no sign of any commercial revival for Slade that year, in spite of releasing a live album and two singles, all of which would flop.

Give Us A Goal single
Personnel:
Noddy Holder: lead vocals, rhythm guitar
Dave Hill: lead guitar, backing vocals
Jim Lea: bass, backing vocals
Don Powell: drums
Studios: Advision, London; Olympic London, 1978
Producer: Chas Chandler
Release date: UK: February 1978
Chart places: UK: –

'Give Us A Goal' (Holder, Lea) b/w **'Daddio'** (Holder, Lea)
With a thunderous rhythm, multitracked handclaps, crowd chants and a huge sing-along chorus, 'Give Us A Goal' was the most unashamed bid to recapture the archetypal Slade sound since the glory days of glam, with Holder cranking out one footballing metaphor after another. Slade had never been particularly linked to the game *per se*, certainly in comparison to uber football fans like Elton John and Rod Stewart – 'I don't even like football', Lea told *Record Mirror* back when the band were passing themselves off as skinheads. However, over the years, many comparisons had been made between the exuberant, chanting crowds attending Slade gigs and those attending football matches. Lea explained the song's origin in a 1991 interview included on the video compilation *Wall of Hits*: 'I wrote this tune, and Nod said, 'Let's do one about football, because we've always had this football following and scarves and 'You'll Never Walk Alone', and always this great empathy with the whole thing about football'. I was never really convinced about doing a football song. Nevertheless, the video was fun'. The video was filmed at Brighton and Hove Albion's football ground, showing the band playing in front of a crowd, interspersed with footage of them having a kickabout with the team.

The B-side 'Daddio' swings along in a shuffle as Holder sings about a duplicitous gambling addict. Though the two sides are very different from one another, it is clear the band had moved on from the much more intense and more serious-sounding heavy rock of *Whatever Happened To Slade*.

Reviewing the single for *Record Mirror*, Rosalind Russell clearly understood what the band were trying to do with all the football analogies, but remained unconvinced: 'It's a bit sad, because I don't think it's worked. I think they're groping in the dark, looking backwards for their future'.

The move back to a more radio-friendly sound was a conscious decision, according to Lea, who told the relaunched Slade fanzine in 1979: 'The releases after *Whatever Happened To Slade* are the songs that got played on the radio – like 'My Baby Left Me', which was a near miss. But it got played on the radio, which is better than being completely obscure, isn't it?'. 'Give Us A Goal' did secure airplay, and slots for the band on the kids' pop shows *Get It Together* and *Cheggers Plays Pop*, but the single failed to reach the top 50.

The single had been released to coincide with a spring UK tour, which included prestigious dates like Hammersmith Odeon in London, and less prestigious ones like the Aquarius Club in Chesterfield. Slade fan Simon Kimmins was at the latter:

Nod was dressed in his checked, tartan jacket and waistcoat, Jim in his leather bomber jacket, Dave with the lights shining off his bald head, and Don topless behind his kit. New music followed – 'Get On Up' – then the difficult to play live 'Be'. The crowd was wild at the front, bemused at the back. The lights were hot and the volume already seemed to be at 11. Nod took off his jacket and looked down at our table and said the stage was so small, he had no room. Could he put the mic stand on our table? He did, and the music continued.

Even if there was little interest from the press beyond the local papers, Slade could still usually rely on a decent turnout to their gigs. But for the Hammersmith Odeon gig on 22 April 1978, both *NME* and *Record Mirror* were out in force to capture the event for their readers. *NME*'s David Blake opted for a back-handed compliment mixed with sneering sarcasm: 'It seems we English take a perverse delight in wasting our best rock singers. Roger Chapman springs to mind, and now Noddy

Holder. Shaved heads and violin solos do not great music make, and it is a shame that a singer of Holder's talent, originality and force is bogged down in such a mire of sound and fury. I guess that's showbiz'.

Reviewing the same gig, *Record Mirror's* Kelly Pike was more complimentary, despite some obvious digs: 'Holder's voice is stronger than ever, with a quality of coarse grit but the strength of an ox. Musically, other than Lea, the band are little-more than competent... I'm not sure I was glad to be taken back, but although Slade are no longer rising stars, they can still pack a punch with their greatest hits, live'.

Following a handful of July dates in Denmark, Slade had an opportunity to tour Poland. The communist authorities had been notoriously sniffy about western rock music throughout the Eastern Bloc, but things gradually began to open up a full decade before the collapse of communism. Touring Poland for three weeks from late July to mid-August, gave Slade a chance to reach fans who had never seen them live, and to play at much larger venues than they had become accustomed to playing back home. But the tour was not without its challenges, as Powell recalled in his biography: 'We all had dysentery. Even the promoter came out in boils. It was like living during the war. You couldn't get the most basic things. When we threw bog rolls into the audience – like we always did during concerts, because it looked great, like big streamers – the audience kept them. They couldn't even get toilet paper there. It was really a bit of an experience, although not always a pleasant one'. But for the Polish fans, it was an unforgettable experience. Slade fan Piotr Szymura attended the concert on 14 August at the Hala Ludowa Hall in Wroclaw – his first and only time seeing the band:

> Slade were like gods for us. In 1978 I was 18, and at that time I had some other idols ... and the punk revolution had just started. But Slade's concert in my city in Poland – at that time behind the Iron Curtain – was like gods stepping down from heaven onto the stage. It was around five, six thousand people inside. I saw hundreds of concerts from 1978, but that one is still in my heart.

On their return from Poland, the band gigged extensively around the UK. Holder wrote in his 1999 autobiography: 'By 1978, we had basically gone back to square one. We were still taking gigs anywhere and everywhere. We still played the occasional concert hall, but we were also doing universities, theatres and even clubs'. The latter was a reference to the series of bookings the band undertook at Baileys nightclubs. These were cabaret clubs, serving food and drink; the entertainment often being well-known performers of a certain vintage. This was the archetypal and much-derided chicken-in-a-basket circuit. Slade performed at Baileys in Watford every night for a week, followed by six nights at a similar club in Leicester, and five nights in Blackburn where Baileys was known as the Cavendish Club. It was a far cry from Earls Court. Early in 1979, *Slade News* asked Powell for his thoughts on playing these clubs: 'Well, it's the best thing, really. Because we were away for so long in the States, we couldn't really expect to go back to the big concert halls because we couldn't fill them. So we went back to doing small places – we knew we could fill those and thus start to build ourselves up again'.

Rock 'N' Roll Bolero single
Personnel:
Noddy Holder: lead vocals, rhythm guitar
Dave Hill: lead guitar, backing vocals
Jim Lea: bass, electric violin, keyboards, backing vocals
Don Powell: drums
Studio: Portland, London, 1978
Producers: Slade ('Rock 'N' Roll Bolero'); Chas Chandler ('It's Alright Buy Me')
Release date: UK: October 1978
Chart places: UK: –

'Rock 'N' Roll Bolero' (Holder, Lea) b/w **'It's Alright Buy Me'** (Holder, Lea)
If Slade's previous single was a conscious return to their classic sound and trademark raunch, the next single pursued a quite different direction altogether. With its piano intro, ghastly syndrum and Lea's electric violin for the first time since 'Coz I Luv You', 'Rock 'N' Roll Bolero' is the sound of Slade trying to keep up with the times, but losing what they are about in the process. It sounded overwrought, over-produced and overly cluttered. It was the first single the band produced themselves, and has the feeling of kids being let loose in a sweet shop and wanting to try a bit of everything. In an interview at the time, Holder told Capital Radio: 'We had a chat with Chas – who has produced all our records for the last nine years – as we felt that we had been getting to a bit of a stalemate.

And Chas said to us that it was about time that we started producing ourselves, or at least getting into the production side of it'.

The B-side – the wonderful 'It's Alright Buy Me' – *was* produced by Chandler, and was vastly superior to the A-side. It remains an unsung Slade classic, with its powerful machine-gun-like bass and life-on-the-road lyric. It showed that the band could deliver memorable hard rock with a modern twist – if only they could find a market for it. It took until the early-1980s to find such an audience – following Slade's spectacular comeback at the Reading Festival – but much of the sonic template for that comeback could be found in this obscure B-side. The French single on Barn Records swapped the A and B sides, but it made little difference.

The *Record Mirror* review at the time was reasonably positive about 'Rock 'N' Roll Bolero': 'A more-mellow Slade here. Gone are the raucous Noddy Holder vocals and the crashing guitars. The fact remains that they're in dire need of a hit, and this could be the one'. But it was not to be. Despite its unashamed commercial pitch, the single received little airplay, failed to secure the TV slots the band were able to get with 'My Baby Left Me' and Give Us A Goal', and failed to chart anywhere. Lea reflected on it in the fan club newsletter in 1979: 'The comment on 'Rock 'N' Roll' Bolero' is that it was different for Slade, but it was ordinary compared to everything else that was around at the time. But I really dig the record myself!'.

Slade Alive, Vol. 2 album (1978)

Personnel:
Noddy Holder: lead vocals, rhythm guitar
Dave Hill: lead guitar, backing vocals
Jim Lea: bass, backing vocals
Don Powell: drums
Recorded on US tour, 1976, UK tour, 1977; Advision Studios, London, 1978
Producer: Chas Chandler
Release date: UK: October 1978
Chart places: UK: -
Running time: 41:01
Tracklisting: Side One: 1. 'Get On Up' (Holder, Lea), 2. 'Take Me Bak 'Ome' (Holder, Lea), 3. 'My Baby Left Me' (Crudup), 4. 'Be' (Holder, Lea), 5. 'Mama Weer All Crazee Now' (Holder, Lea)
Side Two: 1. 'Burning In The Heat Of Love' (Holder, Lea), 2. 'Everyday'

(Holder, Lea), 3. 'Gudbuy T' Jane' (Holder, Lea), 4. 'One Eyed Jacks With Moustaches' (Holder, Lea), 5. 'Cum On Feel The Noize' (Holder, Lea)

> If I wrote songs as bad as this, I'd commit suicide.
> (Dave McCullough, *Sounds* review of *Slade Alive, Vol. 2*, November 1978)

Ostensibly a follow-up to *Slade Alive!*, *Slade Alive Vol. 2* was drawn from a mixture of US shows in 1976 and a gig at the Ipswich Gaumont on 28 May 1977. While there was some overdubs in the studio, it appears that some of the tracks were recorded *entirely* in the studio, with audience applause added afterwards. No matter – the album was a good representation of Slade's live act at the time, with two songs from the recent *Whatever Happened To Slade* album ('Be' and 'One Eyed Jacks'), two recent singles ('My Baby Left Me' and 'Burning In The Heat Of Love') and old favourites like 'Take Me Bak 'Ome' and 'Mama Weer All Crazee Now'.

The cover has live band photographs by Alex Agor, set in (for the time) futuristic-looking graphics. It was the first time Gered Mankowitz' work had not graced a Slade album since the original *Slade Alive!* in 1972. But unlike that album, this one failed to chart at all.

The *Superpop* review deemed the album to be 'a neat little package', arguing that 'Slade have been one of the busiest live bands on the scene recently, and this LP shows exactly what is going on. Somewhat unknown today … but times change, and believe it or not, Slade have'. Not all of the few publications that bothered to review the album were as complimentary, however. By now it was pretty common for reviewers to slag-off new Slade material. But *Sounds'* Dave McCullough, a punk writer determined to metaphorically annihilate anything that did not adhere to his 'Year Zero' mindset, took aim at the old material, too: 'Mama Weer All Crazee Now' is so dire, it's not true. It's got nothing, no hook, no rock-and-roll spirit. If I wrote songs as bad as this, I'd commit suicide. As for 'Gudbuy T' Jane', I feel a chill creep down my back if I'm in the same room as it, y'know? … 'Cum On Feel The Noize' (Jesus Christ almighty) is the pit of pits'.

Despite the reviews, Slade carried on gigging throughout October and November. Once the Baileys engagements were over, they played the usual mix of universities, polytechnics and smaller-sized music venues. *Sounds* were one of the UK papers that enthused about Slade's

Reading Festival comeback two years later, and (along with their sister publication *Kerrang!)* were to become real Slade champions. But back in 1978, *Sounds'* Phil Sutcliffe was in no mood to say anything positive. He reviewed the 20 October Newcastle Polytechnic gig: 'In the darkness, hundreds of people were chanting, 'We want Slade!'. These days, the sad question to be asked is 'Why?'. They may have gone down slow, but they have at last got there – to the bottom of the barrel. The sound of them scraping it for an hour or so at Newcastle Poly, could in no sense be described as music to my ears'.

Not all the reviews were quite so dripping in venom. Some of Slade's most-noteworthy gigs of the late-1970s were at Camden's Music Machine – a former theatre opened on Boxing Day 1900, since renamed KOKO. *Melody Maker* and *Record Mirror* were at the venue on 30 October. While Harry George's *Melody Maker* review alluded to the band's recent foray into the cabaret-club circuit, he was enthusiastic: 'Slade gave a totally authoritative display of rock-'n'-roll rifferama', concluding, 'With a hit single and album, they'd leave most mainstream rockers so far down the field you'd have to pump air into 'em'. Sheila Prophet of *Record Mirror* – who was notably cold the year before following Slade's return from the US – was now somewhat more enthusiastic: 'We've got back the Slade we knew and loved – well, almost. Their stage show still smacks of nostalgia – the new material does not compare well. Of course, Slade could keep on churning out the old stuff till either Noddy's vocal cords or Dave Hill's boots wore out, but sooner or later they'd run out of audience'.

Slade had made it through another year. They were still a working unit and still gigging, whether it was Northern cabaret clubs or Polish stadiums. But they approached 1979 still with no sign of a new hit, and without even the benefit of a deal with Polydor anymore, the label that had played such a crucial role in the band's success. The arrangement for Slade's singles to be released on Chandler's Barn Label via Polydor distribution had now come to an end, and Chandler was obliged to look elsewhere. 1979 was looking tricky, to say the least.

Chapter Eleven: 1979 – Returning To Base

Slade would spend the final year of the 1970s doing pretty much what they did at the start of the decade – releasing an album that would fail to have any chart impact, putting out singles that would not sell, and continuing a relentless schedule of live gigging, all to little or no media fanfare.

January 1979 at least saw the launch of a new Slade fanzine – the old Slade Fan Club having fizzled out at the end of 1977. The fanzine was started by lifelong fan Dave Kemp, who sadly passed away in December 2020, but had painstakingly built an online archive of all the old newsletters at *www.sladefanclub.com*: Here he explains the thinking that led him to set up a new fanzine:

> Slade were now touring heavily in the UK, and I was getting to see lots of gigs. However, there was virtually no information about the band in the music press. Me and other fans would often pass on details of impending record releases and gigs by word-of-mouth. I complained to the band – and in particular Jim Lea – that it was very shortsighted of Chas Chandler to have closed the fan club. It was an ideal medium for the fans to find out the latest info. Jim explained that the Fan Club had become unprofitable. Membership had dwindled, and it was costing more to run than income that was being received in membership fees. However, I kept banging on that it needed to be reinstated. After one gig, Jim said to me, 'Look, Dave, you come to all the gigs, you're in touch with us – if you want a Fan Club, then you run it'.

In late February, the band were back at Baileys, with residencies at Blackburn, Leicester and Watford. The new fanzine *Slade News* reported on one of the Leicester gigs in its March/April edition: 'The audience were not the usual Slade crowd. They were older than the usual fans, and dressed for a night out at a cabaret show – but little did they know!'. Later in that same edition, Lea commented: 'We were offered to come back to do these Baileys clubs. We didn't want to do them in the first place, but we've returned and drawn twice as many people as the first time we appeared here. Playing here for a week in Watford alone means we are going to play to 14,000 people. Whereas, if we did a one-nighter at the college, we would only play to 1,000, even if it was sold out!'.

NME's Steve Clarke reviewed the band at one of the Baileys nights in Watford. Rather than piling on the pathos, his review was extremely positive, ending on a note of optimism about the band's future: 'Visually and musically, they were tight and exciting; Hill and Jim Lea swapping stage positions with energetic dexterity. In the final analysis, there is little real difference between Slade and Status Quo or Thin Lizzy, and it could be that a hit single would shoot them back to the top. But it could also be that they are designed to remain in the shade for the rest of their natural. Time will tell'. Time would tell, indeed. In late March and throughout April, there was more European touring, with gigs in Germany, a second visit behind the Iron Curtain (this time Yugoslavia), and a couple of dates in Austria. German fan Steff Decker was at the Wartburg Music Hall in Weisbaden, Hess, and gave a full concert report for the May/June edition of *Slade News*: 'Although the Wartburg Music Hall is not very large (it holds only 1,000-1,100 people) the voice of the crowd was deafening. Slade played very loudly – louder than when I saw them in Frankfurt in 1977'.

Ginny Ginny single
Personnel:
Noddy Holder: lead vocals, rhythm guitar
Dave Hill: lead guitar, backing vocals
Jim Lea: bass, backing vocals
Don Powell: drums
Studio: Portland, London, 1979
Producer: Slade
Release date: UK: May 1979
Chart places: UK: –

'Ginny Ginny' (Holder, Lea) b/w **'Dizzy Mama'** (Holder, Lea)
The band's first single of 1979 – about a young woman who knows exactly what she wants from life and 'ain't the kind of girl a man can tie down', was a slice of pop-rock that sought to deliver a contemporary update on the typical Slade sound, while still being recognisably them.

The B-side 'Dizzy Mama' opted for hard-hitting rock-and-roll boogie, and became a popular fixture in the band's live set. 'Dizzy Mama' did not appear on the forthcoming *Return To Base* album, but it did make a welcome return on the 1981 album *We'll Bring The House Down*, where it fitted in perfectly.

NME was not sold on 'Ginny Ginny', but at least it got a review: 'Another stab at stardom from the once-superb Slade. A lot better than previous comeback attempts, but still not quite strong enough to compete with other chart contenders, I fear'.

Though released on Chandler's Barn label, it was the first Slade single distributed independently, now that their deal with Polydor had come to an end. Chandler stated in *Slade: Feel The Noize*: 'I tried every record company in London, and nobody wanted to know about Slade'. In the end, Chandler adopted the tactic employed by punk and new-wave bands: 'I found a factory, and pressed-up about 5,000 singles. But they didn't sell at all. In the end, most of them were melted down'. Therefore there was no return to the charts with this single, despite an attempt to make it more eye-catching by pressing it on bright yellow vinyl.

On their return from mainland Europe at the end of April, Slade commenced another UK tour over May and early June, at the usual mix of colleges, clubs and small theatres. But in summer 1979, the band had a return to prominence in the national press. Rather than it being related to the forthcoming album or announcing the next tour, however, the coverage was about a recent court case where a nightclub bouncer was jailed for attacking Holder after a 1978 gig in Porthcawl, South Wales. The *Daily Express* reported on 3 July: 'A rave-up at a pop concert, ended with singer Noddy Holder of Slade nursing a broken nose, a court heard yesterday. It was all due to club bouncers being too aggressive with fans, the 29-year-old pop star claimed'. After Holder had reprimanded bouncers from the stage, one of them had followed him out after the concert, and attacked him. The bouncer in question – Desmond Brothers – was found guilty and was jailed for three months.

Return To Base album (1979)
Personnel:
Noddy Holder: lead vocals, rhythm guitar
Dave Hill: lead guitar, backing vocals
Jim Lea: bass, piano, synthesizer, backing vocals,
Don Powell: drums, percussion
Studio: Portland, London, 1979
Producers: Slade; Chas Chandler ('My Baby's Got It')
Release date: UK: October 1979
Chart places: UK: -
Running time: 33:48

I'm very satisfied with it. It's got a mixture of different types of songs on it, all of which adds up to it being a good album.
(Dave Hill, *Slade News*, November/December 1979)

After touring consistently throughout the first half of 1979, the band spent the summer completing their eighth studio album. *Return To Base* was the first of several Slade albums to be recorded at Portland Studios in Portland Place, central London. The studios were originally established as IBC Recording Studios in the 1930s. They were initially for radio use, but over time it was music production that became the mainstay of the business. By the late-1960s, IBC was regarded as one of the leading London studios. But in 1978, the IBC complex was purchased by Chas Chandler and renamed Portland.

At its heart, *Return to Base* had two distinct personalities. On the one hand, there were the chilled, mellow and sometimes altogether-quite-thoughtful tracks like 'Don't Waste Your Time (Back Street Star)', 'I'm Mad' and 'Sign Of The Times'. On the other hand, there were punchy, hard-hitting rockers like 'Hold On To Your Hats', 'Nuts Bolts And Screws', 'My Baby's Got It' and the Chuck Berry cover 'I'm A Rocker'. This rockier sound came to define the two 1981 albums that followed the band's post-Reading comeback: *We'll Bring The House Down* and *Till Deaf Do Us Part*. Indeed, six of the *Return To Base* tracks ended up being recycled for the former. For this reason, *Return To Base* tends to get overshadowed by its better-selling successor, but it remains a fine album in its own right. What unites both albums' tracks are the strong, memorable melodies that are always at the heart of a good Slade song. *Return To Base* shows a band going through hard times but with a stubborn determination to succeed.

The album appeared in a plain red cover with the words RETURN TO BASE....SLADE appearing along the top in a rough and ready typeface. The album title comes from a line in the song 'Sign Of The Times'. Hill explained in the newsletter: 'It should be a very basic cover, so that it ties in with the *basic* reference in the title'.

'Wheels Ain't Coming Down' (Holder, Lea)
In Holder's second biography *The World According To Noddy*, he explains what inspired this song, saying it was 'about one of the scarier aspects of jetting around the world, when the landing wheels on the plane wouldn't come down, and we had to head off to San Francisco

airport – where the runway is surrounded by sea – to prepare for a crash landing'.

One of Slade's great rock songs, the track opens with the sound effect of a plane soaring across the sky and then Lea's bass emulating the ominous thud-thud-thud of a propellor engine, with keyboards later emulating the sound of a fairground carousel. Together, they perfectly capture the emotional roller coaster of a close brush with death, and the feeling of euphoria when 'you realise you're gonna just survive/It's good to be alive'. The track reappeared on the six-track, 12" EP *Six Of The Best* in 1980, and on the *We'll Bring the House Down* album in 1981, and was released as a single in the UK that year.

'Hold On To Your Hats' (Holder, Lea)
This mid-tempo track is packed with chanted choruses, mean-sounding guitar riffs and pounding hard rock. It reappeared on *We'll Bring The House* Down, and was also that title track's B-side when it was released as a single.

'Chakeeta' (Holder, Lea)
The pop/rock of 'Chakeeta' is one of two tracks that fit neither the hard-and-heavy nor the light-and-mellow templates that characterise the rest of the album – the other track being 'Ginny Ginny' which was a single earlier in the year.

'Don't Waste Your Time (Back Seat Star)' (Holder, Lea)
The first of the album's really mellow tracks has acoustic guitar and Lea's keyboard prominent in the mix. The lyric reflects on the life of a groupie 'riding in them rock-and-roll cars'. Rather than a celebratory tale of rock and roll debauchery, however, this melancholy song would appear to be more of a cautionary tale of the of the is-it-all-worth-it variety. The track reappeared on the six-track 12" EP *Six Of The Best* in 1980.

'Sign Of The Times' (Holder, Lea)
One of the album's mellower songs, this lyric focuses on the 1970s drawing to a close, with Holder – like on the Christmas single – looking to the future. But the future in question here is one marked by fast-moving technological change. The track would also a single in the same month the album was released, and was the B-side of the 'Lock Up Your Daughters' single in 1981.

'I'm A Rocker' (Chuck Berry)

While the original version had a typical Chuck Berry riff, it wasn't one of his most famous songs, but appeared on his 1970 album *Back Home*. Slade inject a huge amount of energy into the song, giving it their classic treatment. In the November/December-1980 *Slade Fan Club* newsletter, Holder explained how it came to be on the album:

> The number came about due to me listening to Annie Nightingale one Sunday afternoon, and she played 'I'm A Rocker' by Chuck Berry. It was one of his new numbers.

After playing it to the others, the band incorporated it into their live set and then recorded it: 'We had half an hour left at the end of the session, and we decided to record it'. It was released as a single in Belgium, and reappeared on the six-track 12" EP *Six Of The Best*, in 1980, and *We'll Bring the House Down* in 1981.

'Nuts Bolts And Screws' (Holder, Lea)

With mean, dirty guitar-playing from Hill and Holder, and a lyric concerning a man's apparent mental-health breakdown, subsequent institutionalisation and resulting sexual frustration, 'Nuts Bolts And Screws' is a superb slice of hard rock that found the perfect home on the better-selling *We'll Bring the House Down* album two years later.

'My Baby's Got It' (Holder, Lea)

Two years after their minor hit with the Elvis Presley tribute 'My Baby Left Me', Slade came up with the similar-sounding 'My Baby's Got It'. A great slice of vintage rock-and-roll boogie with pounding piano and campy choruses, it was reused as the B-side of 'Okey Cokey' later in the, but finally found a worthy home on the *We'll Bring the House Down* album in 1981.

'I'm Mad' (Holder, Lea)

One of the album's most charming tracks, and one of Slade's best slow songs of this era, 'I'm Mad' tracks a man's 'strange exotic dreams'. They are almost certainly drug-induced, given some of the lyric's heavy hints. It shows Slade could still turn out a really beautiful ballad. Out of keeping with the hard and heavy nature of *We'll Bring The House Down*, it was kept *off* that album, but ended up being reused as the B-side of 'Knuckle Sandwich Nancy' in 1981.

'Lemme Love Into Ya' (Holder, Lea)
With its otherworldly sound effects and slow, hypnotic introduction, this track is very un-Slade-like, though Holder's vocal and Hill's gorgeous lead guitar playing make it a magnificent hard rock ballad, and it became a regular feature in concert at the time. Retitled 'Poland' – after the country where the melody was originally conceived – Lea reimagined the song as a piece of light synth-pop for his solo side-project The Dummies. The Slade version reappeared on *We'll Bring the House Down*.

'Ginny, Ginny' (Holder, Lea)
The first single of 1979 was also included on the album.

Reviewing the album for *Record Mirror*, James Parade was complimentary about some of the rockier tracks, but overall remained unimpressed: 'On 'Nuts Bolts And Screws' and 'My Baby's Got It', Slade start to rock, but there's nothing here to distinguish them from any other rocking combo. I wasn't expecting another 'Cum On Feel the Noize' or 'My Friend Stan', but just something a little more inspired. From a new band, this would be a fairly good debut; from Slade, I want more'. The *NME*'s Max Bell was in no mood to be complimentary or, judging from the tone of the review, even to have listened to the album in the first place:

Slade always were a poor man's hard-rock band, appealing to the worst boys-night-out instincts. In the days when bad glam rock was the British norm, this sort of muck might have fitted the bill a treat. But in 1979, who wants to hear a bunch of pathetic old Flash Harrys reiterating the limitations of their puerile sordid imaginations? Haven't these people heard of social security?'

Independently released and distributed, the album barely sold at all in the UK and, unsurprisingly, failed to reach the charts. However, thanks to airplay on a Belgium rock radio station, it became extremely popular as an import, and was subsequently released there by WEA, who also released 'I'm A Rocker' as a single.

Sign Of The Times single
Personnel:
Noddy Holder: lead vocals, rhythm guitar

Dave Hill: lead guitar, backing vocals
Jim Lea: bass, backing vocals
Don Powell: drums
Studio: Portland, London, 1979
Producer: Slade
Release date: UK: October 1979
Chart places: UK: -

'Sign Of The Times' (Holder, Lea) b/w **'Not Tonight Josephine'** (Holder, Lea)

This mellow, futuristically-themed track from *Return To Base* was simultaneously released. It was recycled as the B-side to the 'Lock Up Your Daughters' single following Slade's post-Reading chart comeback in 1981.

The B-side was the considerably faster and more-hard-rocking 'Not Tonight Josephine'. Based on the famous line supposedly attributed to Napoleon turning down his wife's affections, the single would also namecheck Cleopatra, Guinevere and Little Queenie from the Chuck Berry number of the same name. While it did not appear on *Return To Base*, it was recycled as the B-side of 'Wheels Ain't Coming Down' in 1981.

The band still picked up the odd press review at this stage, but *Melody Maker* were far from impressed:

Poor old Slade. Banished by the fickle finger of public taste, they've been hovering in a sort-of no-man's-land for ages. This one won't recapture an audience, even though they're clearly aiming for the ELO sector. Echoed vocals, lots of bombast and the odd *electronic* gimmick do not make a great single. Only when Noddy Holder recaptures his perfect John Lennon imitation will they rise from the ashes.

In the autumn, Slade commenced another UK tour, which ran throughout October. They played the usual mix of colleges, clubs and small theatres. Mike Gardner of *Record Mirror* caught up with the band when they returned to Camden's Music Machine on 20 October:

The oldies like 'Take Me Bak 'Ome', 'Look Wot U Dun', 'Gudbuy T' Jane' and 'Mama Weer All Crazee Now' all sounded even fresher than my memory led me to expect. The tracks from their new album *Return*

To Base sounded equally interesting. Slade are as good a slice of text-book loud, raucous, rowdy, rock-'n'-roll spirit as you are likely to see. It's time for a revaluation of Slade, and it might as well start with you. I advise you to come and feel the noise soon.

There were a handful of December dates, including a return to the Music Machine.

Sadly, in the late-1970s, tensions had continued to mount between Chandler and the band. At one point, Chandler even suggested that Holder and Lea dispense with Hill and Powell, continue as a duo and recruit other musicians. Hill's biography records this as happening in mid-1978 prior to the Poland tour, but Holder and Powell's books place it in late-1979. No matter – Holder and Lea did not act on Chandler's suggestion, and the band continued, though tensions with Chandler would never be properly resolved for as long as he continued to manage the band.

Okey Cokey single

Personnel:
Noddy Holder: lead vocals, rhythm guitar
Dave Hill: lead guitar, backing vocals
Jim Lea: bass, backing vocals
Don Powell: drums
Studio: Portland, London, 1979
Producers: Slade ('Okey Cokey'); Chas Chandler ('My Baby's Got It')
Release date: UK: December 1979
Chart places: UK: -

'Okey Cokey' (Kennedy) b/w **'My Baby's Got It'** (Holder, Lea)
Slade ended the decade with this failed attempt at another Christmas hit. Originating from an 1800s traditional song but copyrighted by lyricist Jimmy Kennedy in the 1940s, 'Okey Cokey' had been a popular music-hall song and a staple of children's parties ever since. Slade crank up the amps and apply their own rocking rhythm to the old novelty-dance song. In fairness, it doesn't sound too bad, and they Sladify as they'd done with numerous other covers in the past. But as a bid to maintain the affection of long-term fans or regain any sort of credibility with the wider public, the single was hopelessly misguided. Hill said in his 2017 book, 'That was a reflection of just how lost we were at that time'.

Certainly, *Record Mirror* was none-too-impressed: 'Yes, it's *that* one. Don't laugh. One day The Clash may be old men singing beer-drinking songs on MFP (Music For Pleasure). Let's hope not'.

The excellent B-side 'My Baby's Got It' came from the recent album. Unsurprisingly, 'Okey Cokey' failed to chart. For their final piece of 1970s promotional work, Slade visited Granada TV studios in Manchester to be filmed miming to 'Okey Cokey' for broadcast on the New Year's Day edition of children's TV show *Get It Together*.

If the story had simply ended there, it would be a sad and rather tawdry end to a wonderful band that had made a massive mark on the music of the 1970s. Of course, it did not end there, and the following year saw one of the most remarkable comebacks of the era.

Chapter Twelve: Bringing The House Down – What Happened Next

The first few months of 1980 were little different from the previous couple of years. There was a UK tour in February and March, a one-off gig in Zurich in April, and a six-track EP came out in May. Titled *Six Of The Best,* it included three tracks from the recent *Return To Base* album and three brand-new tracks: all for the bargain price of just £1.49. However, like pretty much everything Slade had released in the previous two years, it failed to sell.

The band undertook a short UK tour in June, but by this stage, their regular crew had been let go, and Jim Lea's brother Frank stepped in as the tour driver. After the tour's last gig – on 28 June at the West Runton Pavilion on the Norfolk coast – it looked like things were finally drawing to a close for Slade. Lea was focused on his side project The Dummies. Holder was looking forward to spending time with his young family. Powell was rehearsing with an outfit called M.P.H. who were hoping to make an album, and he was also doing session work with singer Sue Wilkinson, who that summer had a hit single with 'You Gotta Be A Hustler If You Wanna Get On', which featured Powell on drums. Of the four band members, Hill had the most eccentric plan for life after Slade, as he recalled in his autobiography: 'I'd still got the gold Rolls Royce, so I had this idea that I was going to go into the wedding-car business – kind of 'Rent a pop star for the big day', driving the bride to the church in a roller'.

Then came a phone call that changed everything. Ozzy Osbourne's post-Black Sabbath outfit Blizzard Of Ozz had been booked to play at the Reading Festival on Sunday, 24 August, but with just a week to go, they had pulled out, citing lack of preparedness. Chandler was approached with an offer for Slade to fill the vacant slot. Holder, Lea and Powell were all keen. Only Hill was reluctant, but in the end, Chandler talked him 'round. Holder recalled in his book: 'As usual, Chas wasn't prepared to take no for an answer. He decided he was going to go up to Wolverhampton to have a word with Dave himself. I don't know how, but Chas talked him into it. I think more-or-less what he said was, 'Do this one show. If you're great or you die on your arse, it doesn't matter. Instead of Slade petering out, end on a high at a festival'. Hill was persuaded, and Slade went to Reading. Hill recalled the triumphant reception the band received: 'We were really good at this point because we had done all the universities, we were gigging regularly, we were ready ... with the years and years of live gigs, we were really at the top of our game and we knocked the crowd sideways: 40,000 people'.

In their festival review for *Sounds*, Geoff Barton and Robbie Millar enthused about Slade's set, arguing that the band 'carried a trophy of trashy magnificence, too powerful for many to reject. Slade were certainly far better than almost all of the HM garbage that'd been thrown at us for most of the weekend', they concluded, with Barton said to be 'in paradise'.

Slade were sounding great, could count on interest from the music press once more and, with the UK's burgeoning heavy metal scene, they found that they had a ready-made audience of younger fans, too. In the introduction to his 2022 book *Denim And Leather: The Rise And Fall Of The New Wave Of British Heavy Metal*, Michael Hann defined this newly-energised scene: 'The new wave of British heavy metal (NWOBHM) encompassed everything from the pop-rock of Praying Mantis to the horrible noise of Venom, and all points in between. Many of the NWOBHM bands had been playing in one form or another for many years before the phrase New Wave Of British Heavy Metal was born'. It was certainly a shot in the arm for the heavy rock scene in the UK, which had been somewhat in the doldrums in the late-1970s. Slade were never silly enough to try and pass themselves off as a NWOBHM band, but the faster, rocked-up versions of their old hits and the new heavier material found instant favour with many NWOBHM fans. Moreover, figures like rock journalist Geoff Barton and radio DJ Tommy Vance were happy to champion both NWOBHM and a revitalised Slade; not to mention the fact that many NWOBHM musicians – now in their late teens and early-20s – had been huge Slade fans in their pre and early teens.

After the lean years, even the more-introverted Lea was more comfortable with public recognition than he had been at the height of the glam years:

I'm a lot more relaxed about the whole thing, whereas back in the day with the band, for a long time, I wasn't. I was better off in the '80s and going into the '90s, but in the '70s, I couldn't cope with all that. If you look at the band, there were two who wanted to get their face in the camera, and two who didn't. And, of course, when we started having hits again in the '80s, it was much easier to cope with because it wasn't that mad teenage chasing-you-down-the-street type stuff.

Touring resumed through autumn and winter 1980, with gigs in the UK and some in mainland Europe. Slade fan Gérard Goyer was at the gig in Lessines, Belgium on 25 October 1980: 'I travelled from Paris to Belgium to see the concert which took place under a marquee. The atmosphere was great with all the fans chanting 'whoa whoa whoa whoa' before and after the concert. This gave Jim Lea the idea for the song 'We'll Bring The House Down'. At the end of the concert, Jim offered me and my brother a beer backstage'.

In the months that followed Reading, Slade were even back in the album chart, albeit with a compilation of old hits. Released by Polydor in November 1980, and aimed at the Christmas market with an extensive TV advertising campaign, *Slade Smashes!* compiled 20 of the band's singles, including all their main hits, and reached 21 in the UK. But two singles released later in the year were less successful. Fortuitously, BBC Radio One had recorded Slade's Reading set for the *Friday Rock Show,* and the band were able to make use of this for two releases on the independent Cheapskate label. The *Alive At Reading* EP brought together three tracks from the incendiary performance – the new song 'When I'm Dancing I Ain't Fighting' and old favourite 'Born To Be Wild' on the A-Side, with a rock-and-roll medley of 'Somethin' Else', 'Pistol Packin' Mama' and 'Keep A Rollin'' on the B-side. The EP only reached 40 in the UK singles chart, but it was Slade's first entry in three years. A second single – utilising live footage from the Reading gig – recycled the studio version of 'Okey Cokey', and spliced it with the crowd sing-along of 'Merry Xmas Everybody' for the A-side, with the wonderfully-memorable rendition of 'Get Down And Get With It' on the flipside. Released as *Xmas Ear Bender*, it reached 70 in the UK singles chart.

Both singles were included on Salvo's 2006 double-disc *Slade Alive!* reissue, but fans would have to wait until 2022 before most of the Reading set enjoyed an official release. The September-2022 *All The World Is A Stage* five-CD box set finally includes the bulk of Slade's legendary performance from the BBC archives, though it omits 'Dizzy Mama', 'My Baby Left Me' and 'Everyday', probably because they were never included in the original BBC broadcast. Holder told *Classic Rock's* Dave Ling in 2022: 'Hearing them all again all these years later, these shows made me realise what a fucking good band we were. I even freaked out at my own vocal prowess. Fucking hell, how did I sing like that for two hours?'.

As 1980 drew to a close, Slade had yet to enjoy another hit single, but the year had witnessed a remarkable turnaround in the band's fortunes. 1981 would be even better. Their return to the UK top ten and the BBC's *Top Of The Pops* came early on during that year. The scene: a suburban lounge in Penwortham on the outskirts of Preston, Lancashire, on 29 January 1981. A family sit down to watch that week's episode of *Top Of The Pops*, and presenter Tommy Vance announces the return of Slade with their new single 'We'll Bring The House Down'.

My mum: 'I didn't know they were still going'.
My stepsister, Ann (aged 16): 'They look a lot older'.
Me (aged 14): 'It's really good though'.

And so began this author's lifelong love affair with the music of Slade. The single in question was a pounding, rabble-rousing slice of hard-rock-cum-heavy-metal that did what some of Slade's most memorable songs had done in the past – it celebrated the loud, raucous energy of a live gig.

Turn the megawatts way up loud
Send an Earth tremor thru the crowd
C'mon, heads down shakin', c'mon

One of the things that makes the track so memorable and made it such a perfect fit for the heavy metal crowd, was Powell's thunderous drum intro. Powell: 'When we recorded that, I just went to the toilet and I made a loud cough, and I thought, 'Ooh, that's a nice echo in here'. And I thought, 'I wonder, how would it be if we put the drums in here?' – because it was all tiled and everything and it was like a thunderous sound in the toilet: absolutely incredible ... I was halfway through this incredible take, and the automatic flush went off'.

The song made its way to number ten in the UK charts and reached 11 in Ireland. A new album, *We'll Bring The House Down* was released in 1981, culling some of the rock tracks from the *Return To Base* album and the *Six Of The Best* EP, along with the current hit single. A hastily-assembled pseudo-compilation it may have been, but it certainly did the trick, allowing Slade to rapidly release new product containing songs the vast majority of buyers would not have heard before. After the success of the *Slade Smashes!* compilation the previous Christmas, the band now demonstrated that they could sell an album of new (or at least new-ish) material, and *We'll Bring The House Down* reached 25 in the UK. But in terms of follow-up singles, things were a little more wobbly. Released in March 1981, 'Wheels Ain't Coming Down' only reached 60 in the UK, and 'Knuckle Sandwich Nancy' – released in May 1981 – did not chart at all. At this point, Slade severed their relationship with Chandler altogether.

The *We'll Bring The House Down* album and its associated singles were released on the Cheapskate label. Jim Lea and his brother Frank originally started the label to release material by The Dummies in 1979, prior to Chandler becoming involved and Slade signing to the label. But by summer 1981, Slade were back on a major label after Chandler negotiated a deal with RCA as one final favour to the band before he stepped down as manager. Not every single on their new RCA label was a major success, but Slade returned to the UK top 30 with 'Lock Up Your Daughters' (29) in 1981, 'My Oh My' (2) in 1983, 'Run Run Away' (7) and 'All Join Hands' (15) in 1984, and one final top-30 hit in 1991 (back on Polydor) with 'Radio Wall Of Sound' (21).

Following *We'll Bring The House Down*, Slade released a further six albums in the 1980s: *Till Deaf Do Us Part* (1981), *Slade On Stage* (1982), *The Amazing Kamikaze Syndrome* (1983), *Rogues Gallery* (1985), *Crackers – The Christmas Party Album* (1985) and *You Boyz Make Big Noize* (1987).

For the first few years after the band's Reading triumph, live work also continued, with the band appearing again at larger venues and some major festivals. A year after Reading, Slade appeared at the Monsters Of Rock heavy metal festival. This time, it was no last-minute booking, and they shared a bill with AC/DC, Whitesnake and Blue Oyster Cult. Carol Clerk wrote in *Melody Maker*: 'The perfect band for this point in the proceedings, Slade came, saw and conquered the whole almighty throng. They chased the challenge of the elements right out of sight. The cold, the wet, the discomfort – nothing mattered'. It was another festival triumph, with your then-15-year-old author among the 65,000-strong crowd. Several years ago, I wrote a blog post reflecting on that day:

In the space of a few months, Slade went from being a band who sang about Christmas – that I vaguely recalled from my childhood – to being my number-one favourite band in the whole world. And that was even before I witnessed what would become (and still remains) the most remarkable live performance I've ever seen. Loud guitar-driven rock, commanding showmanship, unforgettable songs and sheer over-the-top-eccentricity, it was an absolute master class in compelling live performance.

On the back of the previous year's Reading appearance, the early-1980s heavy-metal crowd really took Slade to heart. Looking back at the setlist from Donington, the songs basically fit into three categories. There were – unsurprisingly – the 1970s hits like 'Gudbuy T' Jane' and 'Cum On Feel The Noize', and there was newer material like 'We'll Bring The House Down' and a sneak preview of their soon-to-be-released single 'Lock Up Your Daughters'. Thirdly, there were the old 1950s rock-and-roll covers, which Slade began playing in their wilderness years of the late-1970s, but retained as the heavy-metal crowd began to embrace them. Though the look could not have been more different, this latter group of songs demonstrates how much late-1950s rock-and-roll and early-1970s glam rock had in common.

But it was Noddy Holder's masterful ability to connect with the 65,000-strong crowd that was perhaps even more memorable than the songs. Witty, irreverent, and on a mission to entertain, no matter what – in spite of the non-stop rain, Holder struck an instant rapport with the huge festival audience in a way that few can. And that's before we even get to the surreal sea of moving objects that danced above the crowd's heads throughout the set. Though ever-more-hostile missile-throwing was to mar a number of festivals around that time, with Slade, it was turned on its head, and rather than being fuelled by aggressive machismo, chucking stuff about became a life-affirming celebration of communal craziness – white-plastic beer bottles full of beer, bundles of hay laid on the ground in an attempt to soak up the mud, packed lunches, burger buns – everything that could be thrown in the air, was thrown in the air. The band of course, joined in, with one toilet roll after another being lobbed into the crowd during 'Mama Weer All Crazee Now'. When the crowd called for 'Merry Xmas Everybody' at the end of the set, Holder told us all that if we wanted it, we would have to sing it ourselves, which is precisely what everyone did.

After Slade finished, soaking wet from rain, beer and mud and covered head-to-foot in hay, we made our way towards the back of the crowd to catch our breath, and I wondered whether I would ever see anything on stage quite so magnificent ever again. There were more fantastic performances to come that day, with memorable sets from Whitesnake and AC/DC (once a completely underwhelming Blue Oyster Cult performance was out of the way). However, even though I've seen many exceptional bands over the years, nothing has ever quite matched the intensity of seeing Slade at Donington.

Hill spoke to *Kerrang!*'s Steve Gett in February 1982 about his own particular memories of that day: 'We started touring again after Reading, and things were gradually starting to build up again. But things really moved after Donington. That gig had a great effect on our career because we were up against the best, and there was a huge audience'.

Slade continued touring through 1981, 1982 and 1983, but despite a further UK tour being advertised, the final date of the band's *My Oh My* tour – at the Royal Court Theatre in Liverpool on 18 December 1983 – was to be the last UK gig from the original Slade. In March 1985, the band were booked to support Ozzy Osbourne on a US tour, but after performing several warm-up gigs, they managed just one concert supporting Ozzy. After this show at Cow Palace in San Francisco, Lea was struck ill with hepatitis, and Slade had to pull out of the tour. It was their last-ever full concert. A further UK tour planned for 1985 was subsequently cancelled. Holder had simply had enough of touring. In *The World According to Noddy*, he explained the thinking behind his decision: 'I had major issues to contend with in my personal life, and the truth is that Slade were not gelling as we had done in the '60s and '70s. It used to be the four of us against the world, but since our career revival in the '80s, personality clashes were beginning to pull us apart'.

In spite of the unfortunate fiasco of the Ozzy Osbourne tour, Slade had at least finally achieved the one thing that had continually eluded them throughout the 1970s: commercial success in America. But their belated US breakthrough was less to do with any post-Reading reaction, and more to do with US metal band Quiet Riot's decision to record 'Cum On Feel The Noize'. Holder told *Kerrang!* in December 1983: 'It's a good version of the song. I don't think Quiet Riot have added anything to the original, but they've updated the sound'. Nevertheless, Quiet Riot's version reached five on the *Billboard* Hot 100, and the album it appeared on – *Metal Health* – went all the way to number one. Renewed awareness of the originators of 'Cum On Feel The Noize' helped Slade achieve that long-awaited US recognition. The singles 'My Oh My' and 'Run Run Away' were both top-40 hits in the US, and the US issue of their album *The Amazing Kamikaze Syndrome* (repackaged as *Keep Your Hands Off My Power Supply*, with a slightly different tracklist) reached 33 in the *Billboard* album chart.

Slade continued making records up until 1987, though after 'All Join Hands' was a top 20 hit in late 1984, the hits pretty much dried up. But one final hit single came in 1991. Polydor were planning the compilation *Wall Of Hits*, and asked Slade to record two new tracks. These were also released as singles. The Holder/Lea songwriting partnership had become inactive by this time, and the chosen songs – 'Radio Wall Of Sound' and 'Universe' – were written by Lea alone. Songs that Hill wrote with Bill Hunt (formerly of ELO and Wizzard) appeared on the B-sides of each. If the singles were successful, a new studio album would be considered. Released in October 1991, 'Radio Wall Of Sound' was a surprise late-renaissance for the band, reaching 21 in the UK. But the second single 'Universe' was a flop, and Slade – or at least Slade in the form of Dave Hill, Noddy Holder, Jim Lea and Don Powell – were no more. Holder told *Vive Le Rock* magazine in 2015: 'I'd been in bands for 30 years; we'd been together as Slade with the same four guys for 25 years. It's a long time – I got fed up of it, basically'.

Slade's former manager, producer and all-around champion Chas Chandler died in 1996. Quoted in a lengthy *Mojo* obituary by former Slade publicist Keith Altham, Holder paid tribute: 'We owed our success to Chas, because he gave us the confidence that was born of his own. He goaded Jim Lea and I into writing, and took us through the bad patches. He was a big man in all senses of the word and the most persuasive man we ever met'.

Following the demise of the original Slade, Holder has maintained a consistently-high public profile in the guise of a media personality and occasional actor. He appeared in all three series of the ITV comedy-drama *The Grimleys*, he played Stan Potter in the special live episode of Coronation Street which was broadcast to mark the show's 40th anniversary, and he played mechanic Mick Bustin in a guest appearance on Peter Kay's *Max And Paddy's Road To Nowhere*. In the 1990s and early-2000s, Holder was also a popular radio presenter, with his own long-running show, first for Piccadilly and then Capital. However, it has been in the domain of the TV chat show and lighthearted panel show that Holder has been in near-constant demand – his easygoing manner and endless supply of anecdotes making him a popular call for TV producers.

After Holder quit, Lea had no interest in continuing with Slade. Though he kept a much lower profile than his former songwriting partner, he continued to make the occasional single, and released the solo album *Therapy* in 2007. That was followed by the six-track EP *Lost*

In Space in 2019. Alongside drummer Michael Tongue and bassist Dave Catlin Birch, Lea played his one-and-only full solo gig, at Bilston's Robin 2 venue in 2002. 15 years later, in 2017, Lea delighted fans at the same venue by picking up his guitar to blast out a handful of Slade songs at the conclusion of the *An Audience With Jim Lea* event. Aware of the limitations of his voice and energy levels following a serious brush with cancer, Lea reflected: 'You'd see these old singers like Frank Sinatra when they're past it, and their voice just cracks up, and I said, 'I can't do that'. And then I got this idea of knocking a few backing tracks up, and I did some vocals to see what it sounded like. But I only did four tracks, and then I thought, 'Hang on, I could play along'. And in this day and age, that was my justification'. More recently, Lea has reconnected with old band-mate Powell, and in 2023 the two even began recording together, once more.

Hill never got to pursue his wedding-car idea. When the original band finally came to an end, he and Powell began touring again, recruited some new musicians and went out as Slade II. An album of new material – *Keep on Rockin'* – was released in 1994, but Hill has largely focused on performing the band's old hits live. The band reverted to the Slade name in 2002 and have continued to tour the UK around Christmas most years, also becoming a popular draw at European festivals and UK oldies weekends. For almost three decades after the demise of the original Slade, Powell worked with Hill in the rebooted version of the band: 'Noddy Holder didn't want to tour anymore, so it was just a matter of looking for things, and Dave Hill and myself were still keen on touring, which we did. And actually, it was great, because we went to a lot of territories like Russia and the old Eastern Bloc, which we couldn't do in the '70s'. Hill became the focus of media attention following a somewhat-acrimonious split with Powell in February 2020. Powell had taken time out of the band following a tendon injury, but Hill subsequently decided to continue with a replacement drummer on a permanent basis.

Powell has pursued a range of other projects in recent years, teaming up with Suzi Quatro and Andy Scott in 2017 for the *Quatro, Scott & Powell* album and associated Australian tour. Also, Powell's side project Don Powell's Occasional Flames have released two albums. Despite some major health scares – including overcoming a stroke, and a bowel cancer operation – Powell has continued to make music with his new outfit, The Don Powell Band, which was formed following his split with Hill, as well as with another outfit, Don & The Dreamers.

All four Slade members are understandably proud of their time with the band, and three of them have published memoirs. Holder was first off the mark with *Who's Crazee Now?* (1999), and he also published *The World According To Noddy: Life Lessons Learnt In And Out Of Rock 'N' Roll* (2014). Powell's recollections – *Look Wot I Dun: My Life In Slade* (written with Lyse Lyng Falkenberg) – were published in 2013, while Hill's autobiography *So Here It Is: The Autobiography* came out in 2017. Interviewing Lea in 2018, I put it to him that many Slade fans would say that the most fascinating and revealing of all would be a Jim Lea autobiography. Lea commented:

> At times, I thought about doing it. In fact, I was probably the first one to think about doing it. That was back in post-Reading days. But there seemed to be a reaction that I shouldn't do that, and that if there was going to be any book, it should be a Slade book, not me. So I just left it, and then Nod did one, which I've never looked at, and Don did one which I've never read either, but it's supposed to be very good, I've heard. The thing is, I'd want to write it myself, rather than sitting down with someone with a tape machine. You'd have to be able to taste it and smell it.

But it is not just books – Slade's records continue to sell in sizeable quantities. In October 2020 – as the UK adjusted to the reality of the coronavirus pandemic – the new Slade greatest hits compilation *Cum On Feel The Hitz* went straight into the UK chart at number eight. This was the band's highest album-chart position since *Slade In Flame* in 1974. Even at the time of their early-1980s comeback – when they enjoyed a second run of hit singles – Slade's albums still generally struggled to reach the top 40. All four members played their part in promoting the album and celebrating its success – albeit separately. Powell said, 'I looked at the CD and I thought, 'Blimey. It ain't bad is it? A nice bit of history there'. But also, when it went back in the charts, I thought everybody had got this stuff, you know! How much further can you go, you know. It is incredible!'.

While there is little chance of seeing the four in a room together any time soon, and zero chance of seeing them all onstage together, each are proud of their legacy, and each, in their own way, continue to fly the flag for Slade. As Lea told the author, reflecting on Slade's success: 'We were something special right from the first few notes we ever played'.

Bibliography

Books

Auslander, P., Performing Glam Rock – *Gender and Theatricality In Popular Music* (University of Michigan Press, 2006)

Charlesworth, C., *Slade: Feel The Noize – An Illustrated Biography* (Omnibus Press, 1984)

Checksfield, P., *Look Wot They Dun – The Ultimate Guide to UK Glam Rock on TV in the 70s* (Self-published, 2019)

Checksfield, P., *Top Of The Pops: The Lost Years Rediscovered 1964-1975* (Self- published, 2021)

Dimery, R., *1001 Albums You Must Hear Before You Die* (Cassell Illustrated, 2016)

Edmondson, I., Selby, C., *The Noize: The Slade Discography – second edition* (Self-published, 2021)

Falkenberg, L., Powell, D., *Look Wot I Dun: Don Powell – My Life In Slade* (Omnibus Press, 2013)

Hann, M., *Denim And Leather: The Rise And Fall Of The New Wave Of British Heavy Metal* (Constable, 2022)

Hill, D., *So Here It Is: The Autobiography* (Unbound, 2017)

Holder, N., *Who's Crazee Now?* (Ebury Press, 1999)

Holder, N., *The World According to Noddy* (Constable, 2014)

Hoskyns, B., *Glam!* (Faber & Faber, 1998)

Philo, S., *Glam Rock: Music In Sound And Vision* (Rowman & Littlefield, 2018)

Pidgeon, J., *Flame* (Panther Books, 1975)

Rees, P., *Robert Plant: A Life* (Harper Collins, 2013)

Reynolds, R., *Shock and Awe – Glam Rock and its Legacy* (Faber & Faber, 2016)

Simonelli, D., *Working Class Heroes: Rock Music And British Society In The 1960s and 1970s* (Lexington Books, 2013)

Tremlett, G., *The Slade Story* (Futura Publications, 1975)

Turner, A.W., *Glam Rock – Dandies In The Underworld* (V & A Publishing, 2013)

Various, *Glam: The Genuine Article – Interviews Reviews Rare Photos* (NME Originals, 2004)

Various, *Vive Le Rock: Glam Annual, Volume One* (Big Cheese Publishing, 2022)

Magazine, Newspaper and Journal Articles

Altham, K., 'Slade: Superyob' (*NME*, Feb 1973)

Altham, K., 'Slade in the USA' (*NME*, Jun, 1973)

Altham, K., 'Slade: Keith Altham gets a sneak preview at the next original Slade Album' (*NME*, Sept, 1973)

Altham, K., 'Obituary: Chas Chandler' (*Mojo*, Sept 1996)

Barnes, K., 'Slade: Santa Monica Civic, Santa Monica CA' (*Phonograph Record*, Jun 1973)

Barton, G., 'S.L.A.D.E. the writing's on the wall' (*Sounds*, Nov 1975)

Barton, G., Millar, R., 'A Riot Of Tight Trousers, guitar poses and gaping mouths' (Live review, *Sounds*, Sept 1980)

Beattie, J., 'Slade rip' (*Record Mirror*, May 1974)

Black, J., 'Slade In Flame' (*Q*, July 1999)

Blake, D., 'Slade: Hammersmith Odeon' (Live review, *NME*, April 1978)

Byrom, S., 'America Slade at Last' (*Record Mirror*, Nov 1975)

Carr, R., 'Slade: Bovver Boys Who Grew Their Hair And Got A Hit' (*NME*, July 1973)

Charlesworth C., 'Chas Chandler: Slade Driver' (*Melody Maker*, Oct 1972)

Charlesworth C., 'Slade, Sensational Alex Harvey Band: Earls Court, London' (*Melody Maker*, July 1973)

Charlesworth, C., 'Slade: alive and well…' (Live review, *Melody Maker*, July 1973)

Charlesworth, C., 'Slade: America Feels The Noize' (*Melody Maker*, Nov 1973)

Charlesworth, C., 'Slade: Ambassador Theater, St. Louis, M.O.' (*Melody Maker*, Feb 1974)

Charone, B., 'Slade's Better Class Of Kidz' (*NME*, Nov 1973)

Clarke, S., 'Slade: Watford Baileys' (live review) (*NME*, March 1979)

Clerk, C., 'Let There Be Rock' (Live review, *Melody Maker*, Aug 1981)

Cox, R., 'Longhair Slade sock the rock' (Live review, *Derby Evening Telegraph*, Dec, 1970)

Cromelin, R., 'Slade: Santa Monica Civic, Los Angeles' (Live review, *Music World*, June 1973)

Cromelin, R., 'Slade at the Starwood' (Live review, *L.A. Times*, April 1976)

Crowe, H., 'Little Slade-of-Hand Magic' (Live review, *The Herald*, Feb, 1973)

Dawbarn, B., 'Singles: Who Buys Them' (*Melody Maker*, Feb 1970)

Diggins, M., 'Interview: Jim Lea – Slade' (The Rockpit, Oct 2020)

DiLorwnzo, K., 'Slade: Not As Crazee As Wee Thought' (*Good Times*, Aug, 1975)

Dome, M., 'The Amazing Kami-Khazi Syndrome' (*Kerrang!*, Dec 1983)

Edmonds, B., 'The Working Class Heroes: Noddy Holder' (*Cream*, Jan 1973)

Gardner, M., 'Slade: Music Machine' (Live review, *Record Mirror*, Oct 1979)

George, H., 'Slade: Music Machine' (Live review, *Melody Maker*, Nov 1978)

Gett, S., 'Deaf But Not Dumb' (*Kerrang!*, Feb 1982)

Guthrie, B., 'A Howling Success' (Live review, *The Herald*, Feb 1974)

Hall, L., 'Slade: New Victoria Theatre' (Live review, *Sounds*, April 1975)

Hart, B., 'Land Of The Rising Slade' (Live review, *Daily Mirror*, March 1974)

Hart, B., 'Taxman Is Forcing Them Out' (*The Sun*, April 1975)

Hoskyns, B., 'All The Young Dudes: The Return of Glam Rock' (*Vogue*, Sept 1998)

Iles, J., 'Slade: Bournemouth Winter Gardens' (Live review), *Record Mirror*, April 1975)

Iles, J., 'America Starts To Feel The Noize' (*Record Mirror*, May 1975)

Ingham, J., 'Slade: Steamroller Rock Knocks 'Em Flat' (*Rolling Stone*, Feb 1973)

Irwin, C., 'Slade: Your Public Is Your Judge' (*Melody Maker*, Oct 1974)

Irwin, C., 'Slade: Bournemouth Winter Gardens' (Live review, *Melody Maker*, April 1975)

Irwin, C., 'Slade: On Their Way Back Ome' (Live review, *Melody Maker*, April 1977)

Johnson, J., 'Slade's fanfare for Europe' (*NME*, Jan 1973)

Kent, N., 'Slade: The Kidz Are All Right' (Live review) (*NME*, July 1973)

Ling, D., 'A Beautiful Noize' (Classic Rock, Nov 2022)

Martini, R., 'Slade's Crazee Nite' (*NME*, April 1974)

Mayne, G., 'Slade Sound Spectacular' (Live review, *Sydney Morning Herald*, Feb 1974)

Merinoff, L., 'Slade's American Offensive' (*Record Mirror*, July 1975)

Merinoff, L., 'New York Gets Slade' (Live review, *Record Mirror*, July 1975)

Meyer, B., 'Slade Starts Afresh In US' (*Sarasota Herald Tribune*, Aug 1975)

Morley, P., 'Noizy Boyz Back on UK Track' (Live review, *Melody Maker*, May 1977)

Partridge, P., "Clapton was the first skinhead!' say Slade' (*Record Mirror*, Oct 1969)

Pike, K., 'Gudbuy To Pain' (Live review, *Record Mirror*, April 1978)

Prophet, S., 'Frayed Slade' (Live review, *Record Mirror*, May 1977)

Prophet, S., 'Slade: Music Machine, London' (Live review, *Record Mirror*, Dec 1978)

Irwin, C., 'Slade: On Their Way Back Ome' (Live review, *Melody Maker*, April 1977)

Punter, G., 'Slade: California Ballroom, Dunstable', (Live review, *NME*, July 1972)

Rockwell, J., 'Slade Rock Group At Schaefer Fete Proves Puzzling' (Live review, *New York Times*, July 1975)

Roxon, L., 'A Rock Critic's Rough and Reddy Life' (*New York Sunday News*, April 1973)

Russell, R., 'Slade Shock: We won't make any money out of this tour' (*Disc*, April 1974)

Shaw, G., 'Slade...Arrive!' (*Phonograph Record*, Nov 1972)

Stewart, T., 'Chuck Berry, Pink Floyd, Slade, Billy Preston, Roy Young Band: Lanchester Arts Festival, Locarno, Coventry' (Live review, *NME*, Feb 1972)

Stewart, T., 'Slade: Ar The Kidz Owt've Site Shock Probe' (*NME*, May 1977)

Stratton, J., 'Why Doesn't Anybody Write Anything About Glam Rock' (*Australian Journal of Cultural Studies*, 1986)

Sutcliffe, P., 'Slade: Newcastle City Hall' (Live review, *Sounds*, May 1977)

Sutcliffe, P., 'Slade: Newcastle Polytechnic' (Live review, *Sounds*, Nov 1978)

Telford, R., 'Slade: Balanced madness' (Live review, *Sounds*, June 1972)

Uncredited writer, 'Slade – Last Tour?' (*Record Mirror,* Feb 1971)

Uncredited writer, 'Open verdict on girlfriend of Slade drummer' (*Birmingham Post*, Jan 1974)

Uncredited writer, 'Slade Slay 'Em!' (Live review, *Sunday Mirror*, April 1975)

Uncredited writer, 'Gudbye Ta Slayed?' (*Top Of The Pops*, May 1975)

Uncredited writer, 'Bouncer Broke My Nose Claims Noddy' (*Daily Express*, July 1979)

Van Matre, L., 'I Say Old Man, Even Slade Admit That It's Noise' (Live review, *Chicago Tribune*, June 1974)

Watts, P., 'The Making Of...Slade's Merry Xmas Everybody' (*Uncut*, Dec 2013)

Webb, J., 'The Pantie Chucking Tour: Slade at Newcastle' (Live review, *NME*, Nov 1972)

Weinstein, R.V., 'Slade at Felt Forum, New York' (Live review, *Rolling Stone*, May 1974)

Williams, R., 'Pop Music Hums Again' (*The Times*, Feb 1972)

Album and single reviews

Billboard, Cashbox, Creem, Daily Express, Disc, Kerrang!, Let It Rock, Melody Maker, Music Week, NME, Phonograph Record, Record Mirror, Rolling Stone, Sounds, Superpop.

DVD and VHS

An Audience With Jim Lea (Jim Jam Records, 2018)
Slade In Flame (Union Square Pictures, 2007)
Wall Of Hits (Polygram, 1991)

Online resources

darrensmusicblog.com
donpowellinterviews.blogspot.com
donpowellofficial.com
geirmykl.wordpress.com
officialcharts.com
rocksbackpages.com
scienceandmediamuseum.org.uk
sladediscography.co.uk
sladefanclub.com
sladeinengland.co.uk
sladelive.weebly.com
sladescrapbook.com
sladestory.blogspot.com
slayed.co.uk fan forum
worldradiohistory.com

On Track series

Alan Parsons Project – Steve Swift 978-1-78952-154-2
Tori Amos – Lisa Torem 978-1-78952-142-9
Asia – Peter Braidis 978-1-78952-099-6
Badfinger – Robert Day-Webb 978-1-878952-176-4
Barclay James Harvest – Keith and Monica Domone 978-1-78952-067-5
The Beatles – Andrew Wild 978-1-78952-009-5
The Beatles Solo 1969-1980 – Andrew Wild 978-1-78952-030-9
Blue Oyster Cult – Jacob Holm-Lupo 978-1-78952-007-1
Blur – Matt Bishop – 978-178952-164-1
Marc Bolan and T.Rex – Peter Gallagher 978-1-78952-124-5
Kate Bush – Bill Thomas 978-1-78952-097-2
Camel – Hamish Kuzminski 978-1-78952-040-8
Caravan – Andy Boot 978-1-78952-127-6
Cardiacs – Eric Benac 978-1-78952-131-3
Eric Clapton Solo – Andrew Wild 978-1-78952-141-2
The Clash – Nick Assirati 978-1-78952-077-4
Crosby, Stills and Nash – Andrew Wild 978-1-78952-039-2
The Damned – Morgan Brown 978-1-78952-136-8
Deep Purple and Rainbow 1968-79 – Steve Pilkington 978-1-78952-002-6
Dire Straits – Andrew Wild 978-1-78952-044-6
The Doors – Tony Thompson 978-1-78952-137-5
Dream Theater – Jordan Blum 978-1-78952-050-7
Electric Light Orchestra – Barry Delve 978-1-78952-152-8
Elvis Costello and The Attractions – Georg Purvis 978-1-78952-129-0
Emerson Lake and Palmer – Mike Goode 978-1-78952-000-2
Fairport Convention – Kevan Furbank 978-1-78952-051-4
Peter Gabriel – Graeme Scarfe 978-1-78952-138-2
Genesis – Stuart MacFarlane 978-1-78952-005-7
Gentle Giant – Gary Steel 978-1-78952-058-3
Gong – Kevan Furbank 978-1-78952-082-8
Hall and Oates – Ian Abrahams 978-1-78952-167-2
Hawkwind – Duncan Harris 978-1-78952-052-1
Peter Hammill – Richard Rees Jones 978-1-78952-163-4
Roy Harper – Opher Goodwin 978-1-78952-130-6
Jimi Hendrix – Emma Stott 978-1-78952-175-7
The Hollies – Andrew Darlington 978-1-78952-159-7
Iron Maiden – Steve Pilkington 978-1-78952-061-3
Jefferson Airplane – Richard Butterworth 978-1-78952-143-6
Jethro Tull – Jordan Blum 978-1-78952-016-3
Elton John in the 1970s – Peter Kearns 978-1-78952-034-7
The Incredible String Band – Tim Moon 978-1-78952-107-8
Iron Maiden – Steve Pilkington 978-1-78952-061-3
Judas Priest – John Tucker 978-1-78952-018-7

Kansas – Kevin Cummings 978-1-78952-057-6
The Kinks – Martin Hutchinson 978-1-78952-172-6
Korn – Matt Karpe 978-1-78952-153-5
Led Zeppelin – Steve Pilkington 978-1-78952-151-1
Level 42 – Matt Philips 978-1-78952-102-3
Little Feat – 978-1-78952-168-9
Aimee Mann – Jez Rowden 978-1-78952-036-1
Joni Mitchell – Peter Kearns 978-1-78952-081-1
The Moody Blues – Geoffrey Feakes 978-1-78952-042-2
Motorhead – Duncan Harris 978-1-78952-173-3
Mike Oldfield – Ryan Yard 978-1-78952-060-6
Opeth – Jordan Blum 978-1-78-952-166-5
Tom Petty – Richard James 978-1-78952-128-3
Porcupine Tree – Nick Holmes 978-1-78952-144-3
Queen – Andrew Wild 978-1-78952-003-3
Radiohead – William Allen 978-1-78952-149-8
Renaissance – David Detmer 978-1-78952-062-0
The Rolling Stones 1963-80 – Steve Pilkington 978-1-78952-017-0
The Smiths and Morrissey – Tommy Gunnarsson 978-1-78952-140-5
Status Quo the Frantic Four Years – Richard James 978-1-78952-160-3
Steely Dan – Jez Rowden 978-1-78952-043-9
Steve Hackett – Geoffrey Feakes 978-1-78952-098-9
Thin Lizzy – Graeme Stroud 978-1-78952-064-4
Toto – Jacob Holm-Lupo 978-1-78952-019-4
U2 – Eoghan Lyng 978-1-78952-078-1
UFO – Richard James 978-1-78952-073-6
The Who – Geoffrey Feakes 978-1-78952-076-7
Roy Wood and the Move – James R Turner 978-1-78952-008-8
Van Der Graaf Generator – Dan Coffey 978-1-78952-031-6
Yes – Stephen Lambe 978-1-78952-001-9
Frank Zappa 1966 to 1979 – Eric Benac 978-1-78952-033-0
Warren Zevon – Peter Gallagher 978-1-78952-170-2
10CC – Peter Kearns 978-1-78952-054-5

Decades Series

The Bee Gees in the 1960s – Andrew Môn Hughes et al 978-1-78952-148-1
The Bee Gees in the 1970s – Andrew Môn Hughes et al 978-1-78952-179-5
Black Sabbath in the 1970s – Chris Sutton 978-1-78952-171-9
Britpop – Peter Richard Adams and Matt Pooler 978-1-78952-169-6
Alice Cooper in the 1970s – Chris Sutton 978-1-78952-104-7
Curved Air in the 1970s – Laura Shenton 978-1-78952-069-9
Bob Dylan in the 1980s – Don Klees 978-1-78952-157-3
Fleetwood Mac in the 1970s – Andrew Wild 978-1-78952-105-4
Focus in the 1970s – Stephen Lambe 978-1-78952-079-8

Also available from Sonicbond

Free and Bad Company in the 1970s – John Van der Kiste 978-1-78952-178-8
Genesis in the 1970s – Bill Thomas 978178952-146-7
George Harrison in the 1970s – Eoghan Lyng 978-1-78952-174-0
Marillion in the 1980s – Nathaniel Webb 978-1-78952-065-1
Mott the Hoople and Ian Hunter in the 1970s – John Van der Kiste
978-1-78-952-162-7
Pink Floyd In The 1970s – Georg Purvis 978-1-78952-072-9
Tangerine Dream in the 1970s – Stephen Palmer 978-1-78952-161-0
The Sweet in the 1970s – Darren Johnson from Gary Cosby collection 978-1-78952-139-9
Uriah Heep in the 1970s – Steve Pilkington 978-1-78952-103-0
Yes in the 1980s – Stephen Lambe with David Watkinson 978-1-78952-125-2

On Screen series
Carry On… – Stephen Lambe 978-1-78952-004-0
David Cronenberg – Patrick Chapman 978-1-78952-071-2
Doctor Who: The David Tennant Years – Jamie Hailstone 978-1-78952-066-8
James Bond – Andrew Wild – 978-1-78952-010-1
Monty Python – Steve Pilkington 978-1-78952-047-7
Seinfeld Seasons 1 to 5 – Stephen Lambe 978-1-78952-012-5

Other Books
1967: A Year In Psychedelic Rock – Kevan Furbank 978-1-78952-155-9
1970: A Year In Rock – John Van der Kiste 978-1-78952-147-4
1973: The Golden Year of Progressive Rock 978-1-78952-165-8
Babysitting A Band On The Rocks – G.D. Praetorius 978-1-78952-106-1
Eric Clapton Sessions – Andrew Wild 978-1-78952-177-1
Derek Taylor: For Your Radioactive Children – Andrew Darlington
978-1-78952-038-5
The Golden Road: The Recording History of The Grateful Dead – John
Kilbride 978-1-78952-156-6
Iggy and The Stooges On Stage 1967-1974 – Per Nilsen 978-1-78952-101-6
Jon Anderson and the Warriors – the road to Yes – David Watkinson
978-1-78952-059-0
Nu Metal: A Definitive Guide – Matt Karpe 978-1-78952-063-7
Tommy Bolin: In and Out of Deep Purple – Laura Shenton 978-1-78952-070-5
Maximum Darkness – Deke Leonard 978-1-78952-048-4
Maybe I Should've Stayed In Bed – Deke Leonard 978-1-78952-053-8
The Twang Dynasty – Deke Leonard 978-1-78952-049-1

and many more to come!

Would you like to write for Sonicbond Publishing?

At Sonicbond Publishing we are always on the look-out for authors,
particularly for our two main series:

On Track. Mixing fact with in depth analysis, the On Track series
examines the work of a particular musical artist or group. All genres
are considered from easy listening and jazz to 60s soul to 90s pop,
via rock and metal.

On Screen. This series looks at the world of film and television.
Subjects considered include directors, actors and writers, as well
as entire television and film series. As with the On Track series, we
balance fact with analysis.

While professional writing experience would, of course, be an
advantage the most important qualification is to have real enthusiasm
and knowledge of your subject. First-time authors are welcomed, but
the ability to write well in English is essential.

Sonicbond Publishing has distribution throughout Europe and North
America, and all books are also published in E-book form. Authors
will be paid a royalty based on sales of their book.

Further details are available from www.sonicbondpublishing.co.uk.
To contact us, complete the contact form there or
email info@sonicbondpublishing.co.uk

Follow us on social media:
Twitter: https://twitter.com/SonicbondP
Instagram: https://www.instagram.com/sonicbondpublishing_/
Facebook: https://www.facebook.com/SonicbondPublishing/
Linktree QR code: